SPOTLIGHT ON CARD PLAY

This book is designed to turn moderately good bridge
players into expert players of the cards, by use of novel and
entertaining methods.

Spotlight on Card Play can be read just for pleasure, for the
many hands in it exemplify what Dr Paul Stern described as
Darvas's 'extraordinary gift for discovering the unusual
features of bridge hands—the beautiful, the bizarre, the
exciting, and even the comical'. Though these hands are
again all that, they are this time also turned to the intensely
practical purpose of making the reader a better *player of the
cards*.

Darvas and Lukacs, in fact, show as in a revealing
spotlight the expert's psychological tricks of the trade and
explain, without explaining away, his seemingly uncanny
insight in finding the right technical device to use on each
occasion. The reader who co-operates with the authors in
the playing of these 67 hands can hardly fail to find life at
once fuller and easier next time he sits down at a bridge
table.

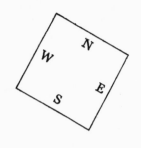

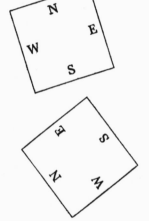

SPOTLIGHT
ON CARD PLAY

A NEW APPROACH TO THE
PRACTICAL ANALYSIS OF
BRIDGE HANDS

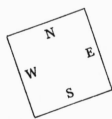

BY ROBERT DARVAS
AND PAUL LUKACS

Foreword by HUGH KELSEY

LONDON
VICTOR GOLLANCZ LTD
in association with Peter Crawley
1982

First published by
Nicholas Kaye Limited
1960
This edition published 1982
Copyright © 1960 Nicholas Kaye Limited
Foreword © Hugh Kelsey 1982

British Library Cataloguing in Publication Data

Darvas, Robert
    Spotlight on card play.
    1. Contract bridge
    I. Title   II. Lukacs, Paul
    795.41'53   GV1282.3

    ISBN 0-575-03078-X

Printed in Great Britain by
St Edmundsbury Press
Bury St Edmunds, Suffolk

CONTENTS

FOREWORD BY HUGH KELSEY

One of the more tedious duties of an editor is to check for errors, so when the plan to reissue *Spotlight on Card Play* was finally agreed, I dug out my battered copy, bought in Kuala Lumpur twenty years ago at a cost of eight Malayan dollars, and sat down at my desk with blue pencil poised. To my astonishment and delight, I could not find a single flawed analysis in the whole book. There was nothing for me to do, and my chore turned into pure pleasure as I rediscovered one magnificent hand after another.

When one considers the credentials of the distinguished Hungarian authors, it is hardly surprising that the book is free from error. Robert Darvas, one of the best-loved, most creative and most entertaining of all bridge writers, had a rare genius for discovering unusual and instructive points of play. His friend and collaborator, Paul Lukacs, the brilliant master of the bridge quiz, has been writing authoritatively about the game for five decades. What is it about the Hungarians, I wonder, that makes them excel as bridge analysts?

Those who have never read Darvas and Lukacs have a great treat in store as they are introduced to the workings of the expert mind and guided through the play and defence of 67 fascinating hands. Those who know the book may rejoice in discovering, as I did, that the deals in this superb collection are as fresh today as they were when they first came out.

INTRODUCTION BY NORMAN DE V. HART

This book breaks fresh ground in two directions. In inviting the reader to play each of the 67 hands to best advantage, my authors place before him only the 26 cards that he would see if he were playing the hand in a rubber—or in a match—at the bridge table. That is a departure from the almost invariable practice followed in books on play of displaying all the 52 cards as dealt to the four players. The other novelty is that the analysis of each hand is carried through by means of questions and answers which conduct the reader step by step to the decisions that have to be made and acted on.

These two distinctive features were not adopted for the sake of novelty, but because my authors found them necessary to the purpose of the book. That purpose is to demonstrate to those myriads of bridge-players who think expert card-play beyond them that, on the contrary, it is quite within their reach if they have any aptitude at all. So many of them bid really well, have the right temperament, and love the game; yet they regard the way experts constantly find and use the technical play appropriate to the situation, set traps for each other, and do card-reading and hand-counting, as little short of magic. They have learned, of course, generally from text-books, the mechanics of the various technical devices—the squeeze and other end-plays, reverse dummy, safety-plays, and the rest. But they have discovered that to know is one thing and to apply their knowledge at the bridge table is something else. It is precisely the expert's know-how that they lack and envy. This book sets out to anatomize the expert's know-how in 67 picked examples.

To do that it was necessary to realize the conditions of actual play as closely as possible; so, obviously, only dummy's cards and those of the hand the reader is supposed to be playing could be visible. And questions and answers seemed the best and most vivid way of showing the expert mind at work: how it approaches each hand, examines the chances and difficulties, and decides on the best course of action. This step-by-step method of analysis, combined with keeping 26 cards out of sight, also has the advantage that hands with several intriguing turns or variations can be introduced and readily coped with.

But the questions and answers are intended to do more than exhibit the expert mind 'doing its stuff'. The questions are an invitation to the reader to think up the answers for himself, and thus to allow his mind to be directed, exercised, and disciplined in the ways of expert thought. That invitation is given explicitly in the first three hands of the book; thereafter it remains implicit. Clearly, the reader who thus co-operates actively in going through the 67 hands is likely to benefit a good deal more than the reader who looks only for the entertainment which the book also aims to provide.

Slams are fascinating and thrilling, and most players nowadays keep on the qui vive for opportunities to bid them. But nothing is more frustrating than the anticlimax of failing to make a well-bid slam for lack of the insight or technique needed to bring it to fruition. Hardly less maddening is it to be in a doubtful, or perhaps even a downright bad, slam and not know how to give oneself the best chance, however slight, of getting away with it. So, while there are many slams in the book, some of them are, intentionally, not at all good contracts.

In short, this is not a systematic handbook on play, with every hand a 'success story', but an attempt to provide fruitful exercise in the reality of things as they can and do happen at the bridge table. Each hand, whether chosen or composed, is intended to illustrate in practical fashion at least one concrete point of play worth storing in the mind. Experience of different kinds of hands, from the ordinary to the strange and perplexing, becomes a potent asset when it has been properly assimilated. Well, here a wide field of experience is concentrated in pre-digested form, ready for assimilation.

Nor is defensive play neglected. In many of the hands the reader is invited to find ways of breaking contracts. Where that is the case, the bidding is always given; but where dummy play is concerned, sometimes only the final contract is mentioned, which means it was reached without either opponent bidding.

The hands are arranged in no particular order, except that the first few hands are relatively simple so as to accustom the reader to the method of gradual analysis. Several hands from actual play are credited to the eminent people who played them.

One final word: Some bridge players find it rather tiresome to visualize card play from diagrams. Their best course is to lay out actual cards on a table. This is no arduous matter when only 26 cards are involved, and is much more like the real thing.

HAND NO. 1
HELP FROM THE BIDDING

♠ K 8 2
♡ A 6 3
◇ K J 4
♣ A 10 7 6

```
        N
   W         E
        S
```

♠ Q J 10 3
♡ Q 4
◇ Q 9 7 2
♣ K 5 3

Both vulnerable. You are South. The bidding:

North	East	South	West
1 ♣	1 ♠	1 N-T	No
2 N-T	No	3 N-T	All pass

West leads the ♡5, dummy plays the Three, East wins with the King, and returns the ♡9. Your Queen takes the trick.

HOW MANY TRICKS HAVE YOU IN PROSPECT?

STOP AND THINK

There are two immediate tricks in Clubs and one more in Hearts. Two Diamond and three Spade tricks can be promoted, making, with the Heart trick you have already, nine tricks in all.

IS THE MAKING OF THESE NINE TRICKS ENDANGERED IN ANY WAY?

STOP AND THINK

Yes, for in setting up your Diamond and Spade tricks you have to let opponents get the lead twice. If they knock out your Heart stopper the first time they have the lead, the next time they get it they may be able to run off two or three Heart tricks.

SO WHICH SUIT DO YOU TACKLE FIRST TO MINIMIZE THE DANGER?

STOP AND THINK

Cast your mind back to the bidding. It is highly improbable that East intervened with a vulnerable bid of Spades on small cards only in the suit. Therefore he can be placed with the ♠A. He may, of course, have both missing aces; but you can't count on that. West may be treasuring the ◇A as an entry for his Hearts. In case that should be so, you lead Diamonds to get the Ace out while you still stop Hearts. You lead a small Diamond towards dummy's King. If opponents refuse to take the first round of Diamonds, you play a second round, leading dummy's Knave. To return to your own hand with the ♣K in order to lead Diamonds towards dummy again would be a fatal mistake for two reasons. First, on getting in with the ◇A, opponents could play Clubs. Secondly, if opponents duck Diamonds twice and similarly wait to take the third round of Spades, there is no entry left to your own hand.

WHAT DO YOU DO IF TWO ROUNDS OF DIAMONDS ARE DUCKED?

STOP AND THINK

Having made the two Diamond tricks you need, you switch to Spades.

A VITAL ENTRY

♠ Q J 5
♡ A 8 3
◇ J 10 4
♣ A 7 5 2

```
        N
  W           E
        S
```

♠ 8 3 2
♡ K 10 7
◇ K Q 6 2
♣ K Q J

You are South, and your contract is Three No-Trumps. West leads the ♡6.

IS THE CONTRACT IN SIGHT?

STOP AND THINK

Yes. You have two tricks in Hearts, three in Diamonds, and four in Clubs, totalling nine.

IN WHAT ORDER DO YOU INTEND TO BRING HOME YOUR TRICKS?

STOP AND THINK

It looks a good idea to play low in dummy so as to take the trick cheaply in South's hand as the Eleven Rule tells you East has no Heart higher than the Six. That would be all right if you could be certain that West has led his fourth highest Heart. But perhaps he hasn't; and then the Rule of Eleven simply won't work, and you may well find your ♡K forced out by the Knave or Queen appearing from East's hand. You next cash South's three high Clubs, enter dummy with a Diamond—for, of course, opponents hold up the Ace—and cash the ♣A. Again you play Diamonds, and the Ace appears only on the third round of the suit. Now there is no entry in South's hand for making the third Diamond trick. You can no longer get nine tricks.

CAN YOU SPOT THE MISTAKE?

STOP AND THINK

The first trick was taken in the wrong hand. You must resist the temptation to assume that West's ♡6 is the orthodox fourth-high lead. In this hand you dare not bank on the Rule of Eleven, and risk having to play your ♡K prematurely. So you take the first trick with dummy's ♡A, and thus ensure the safety of your ♡K as entry to your hand for the third essential Diamond trick after you have cashed your four Club tricks in the way already described. That makes your contract nearly a certainty.

WHY ONLY NEARLY? IS THERE A DISTRIBUTION OF THE OPPOSING CARDS THAT CAN DEFEAT YOU?

STOP AND THINK

There is. If either opponent has six Clubs and a convenient entry, declarer can lose two Clubs, two Spades, and one Diamond. The probability of this is less than one per cent. But suppose it does happen that either opponent fails to follow to the first round of Clubs.

WHAT DO YOU DO ABOUT IT?

STOP AND THINK

Nothing. You simply play on as planned. For in spite of the 6–0 Club break there are still some chances in your favour.

WHAT ARE THEY?

STOP AND THINK

(1) The ◇A is singleton or doubleton. (2) The defence slips up by taking the first or second round of Diamonds. (3) The defence makes some other mistake. (4) The opponent with the Clubs has no entry. (5) Spades are blocked.

CREATING A DILEMMA

♠ 8 3
♡ A 7
◇ A Q J 6 4 3
♣ 7 5 2

♠ K Q J 10 6 4
♡ 6 5 2
◇ 8
♣ A K 6

You are South, and your contract is Four Spades. West leads the ♡K.

WHAT HAPPENS IF YOU TAKE WITH THE ACE?

STOP AND THINK

If you return Hearts, opponents take the trick and strip dummy of trumps by playing the ♠A and another Spade. Then you are left with the Diamond finesse—a poor 50 per cent chance. If you cash the ◇A and lead another Diamond honour, that is still worse. Now you lose your contract anyway.

IS THERE NOTHING BETTER THAN THE DIAMOND FINESSE?

STOP AND THINK

Duck the opening lead, and you have a very good chance of making your contract. The whole picture has changed. If opponents now take out dummy's trumps, you draw the remainder and then play out the ◇A and ◇Q—the best way to handle the suit. You ruff if the Queen is covered; if not, you discard your losing Club. In this way you make five Spade tricks, one Heart, two Diamonds, and two Clubs. If West shifts to Clubs at the second trick, take your Ace and lead the ♠K. If opponents take it and return a black suit, you have no problem. But suppose opponents lead a red suit either then or at the second trick, or suppose they refuse to take the ♠K.

HOW DO YOU ACT IN THESE CASES?

STOP AND THINK

In all these cases the tenth trick must come from a Heart ruff. The chance of its success is about 70 per cent. If Diamonds are led by West, you don't finesse, of course, but go up with the Ace, cash the ♡A, and return to your hand with a Club to take the Heart ruff with dummy's ♠8.

You solved the mild complications of this hand, as you will find you can often solve much more difficult situations, by making a *waiting move*. When you ducked the first trick, you presented West with a dilemma—either to leave you an entry in dummy for the Diamonds, or to let you ruff a Heart.

HAND NO. 4
SAFETY FIRST

♠ 9 5 2
♡ 8 4 2
♢ 8 6 3
♣ A K 7 4

```
        N
   W         E
        S
```

♠ A K 4
♡ A Q J 10 9
♢ J 4
♣ Q J 2

You are South, and your contract is Four Hearts. West attacks with Diamonds, and you ruff the third round. The situation is promising. Seemingly only a trump trick can be lost, since South's losing Spade can be thrown on dummy's fourth Club. The first thing, of course, is to get trumps out.

HOW DO YOU SET ABOUT DOING THAT ?

You could finesse against the King; and if it is with East, singly or doubly guarded, you make your contract and quite possibly an overtrick. This plan, however, is quite unsound.

WHY IS IT UNSOUND?

To take the finesse you must use up at least one of dummy's high Clubs; and if that suit does not break 3–3, you may lose a trump trick and a Spade, since you have to overtake one of your own Club honours in order to get to the table, and so would have no way to rid yourself of your losing Spade. This reckless play endangers your contract if the opposing Clubs are unevenly divided. For West may have the ♡K and refuse to take the first round of trumps. You cross to dummy, using up its second Club honour, and the trump finesse loses on the second round.

Trump finessing is often bad. Here, playing the ♡A and another Heart is much better, as it catches the ♡K if it is single and is also winning play if neither opponent has four trumps to the King. Against that holding you may make your contract again only if the Clubs break 3–3; for you cannot play trumps endlessly because of the danger of being shortened by a Diamond lead when dummy runs out of trumps.

SO WHAT IS REALLY THE BEST WAY TO HANDLE THE TRUMP SUIT?

At the fourth trick, when you have ruffed the third round of Diamonds, lead the ♡Q. If the King takes and neither opponent is void, your contract is safe. Dummy's ♡8 protects you from trump-shortening, and you can draw all the outstanding trumps. If the ♡K is held up, continue with the Knave. If the King now takes, again all is well. If the King is still held up and West shows out, you cross to dummy with a Club and pick up East's still-guarded King.

CAN YOU STILL MAKE YOUR CONTRACT IF WEST HOLDS FOUR TRUMPS TO THE KING?

Yes, if West also has three Clubs. You cash the ♡A and the top Clubs, and throw your losing Spade on dummy's fourth Club which West can only trump with his now bare King.

In this hand you refrained from playing for an overtrick in order to guard against an unfavourable (here 4–1) trump distribution.

HAND NO. 5

A CASE FOR CAUTION

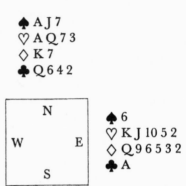

♠ A J 7
♡ A Q 7 3
◇ K 7
♣ Q 6 4 2

♠ 6
♡ K J 10 5 2
◇ Q 9 6 5 3 2
♣ A

East-West vulnerable. You are East. The bidding:

North	East	South	West
1 ♡	No	1 ♠	No
2 ♠	No	4 ♠	All pass

West leads the ♡4, dummy's Queen is finessed, and you make your King, South playing the ♡9.

WHAT DOES THE FIRST TRICK TELL YOU?

That West's lead was probably a singleton. If so, South has false-carded. As you can see the ♡2 and ♡3, the Four was West's only Heart, as he would be unlikely to lead that from ♡8-6-4 or from a doubleton. Therefore the declarer had ♡9-8-6, and risked nothing by dropping the Nine in an attempt to inhibit a Heart return, which he evidently fears either because of the ruffing danger or because he does not want dummy's ♡A to be driven out and the suit established for East-West. The conclusion you draw is that the defence must be based on Heart ruffs.

SO WHAT DO YOU LEAD AT THE SECOND TRICK—A HEART OR THE ACE OF CLUBS?

The cashing of the ♣A would give you a Club ruff when West returns that suit after trumping a Heart. But that plan runs the risk of being upset by South having a singleton Club, in which case you cannot get the lead again to give West a second Heart ruff that might well prove to be the setting trick. So we advise you to be pessimistic about Clubs, and to return Hearts at once.

AND WHICH HEART DO YOU LEAD?

Some players might lead the ♡J or ♡10 to establish the suit if West, for some reason, does not ruff. But in the present situation the lead of a high Heart would inevitably be interpreted by West as a McKenney suit-preference signal telling him to return the higher-ranking of the two remaining side-suits, namely Diamonds —the very last thing you want. So the correct lead is the ♡2, asking your partner to return the lower-ranking side-suit— Clubs. When he does so and you make your ♣A, you now lead the ♡5—plainly your lowest Heart, asking again for a Club return.

This hand shows the importance of maintaining contact with your partner—first, by refusing to risk the cutting of your Club communications; secondly, by taking care to signal correctly to him.

HAND NO. 6
A POSITIONAL MOVE

♠ 9 7 4
♡ Q 4
♢ Q 10 7 2
♣ A 6 3 2

```
        N
   W         E
        S
```

♠ A K J 8 3
♡ 10 9 5 3
♢ 4
♣ K 8 5

Both vulnerable. You are South. The bidding:

East	South	West	North
1 ♡	1 ♠	No	No
2 ♢	No	No	2 ♠
All pass			

West leads the ♡7, dummy plays the Four, and East takes the trick with his Knave. He leads the ♠10, and you win with the Ace.

And now, just this once, don't 'stop and think'. Take a cursory glance at the situation, and then decide, without further thought, what you feel, intuitively, is the best lead for you to make.

Assuming you have made your quick, unreflective decision, we now go on to analyse the hand in the usual way.

WHAT INFORMATION HAVE YOU OBTAINED FROM THE BIDDING AND FROM THE PLAY OF THE FIRST TWO TRICKS?

East originally held nine or ten red cards—probably five Hearts and four or five Diamonds. So he probably only had one or two of your trumps. His Hearts were headed by the Ace-King-Knave, and in Diamonds he is likely to have only one high honour, or he would have bid more strongly.

IF EAST HAS ONE TRUMP LEFT NOW, HOW DO YOU PLAN TO PLAY?

To set up a Heart trick by letting East make three tricks with his Ace-King-Knave. This enables you to discard two of dummy's Clubs, and eventually you ruff a Club in dummy.

DO YOU, THEN, PLAY A HEART IMMEDIATELY?

No. East would win, and play trumps again. If you then led another Heart, East could give West the lead with a Diamond, and West would then cash ♠Q, and away goes your Club ruff.

CAN YOU DO ANYTHING TO PREVENT THIS HAPPENING?

Yes, by an immediate Diamond lead, now, at the third trick. This cuts the defence's communications, and your plan cannot be interfered with. If West should assert himself with his trumps at any stage, you get a trump trick in place of the Club ruff.

But suppose East had only one trump originally, and so has none left now after his trump lead at the second trick.

HOW DO YOU PLAN TO PLAY IN THAT CASE?

Your plan of letting East make his high Hearts would no longer work, as West could trump your established Heart without unguarding his ♠Q. The best thing to do is to cross-ruff Hearts and Diamonds; and the way to start that operation is again an immediate Diamond lead.

We believe that a player with a good card-sense needs no more than a superficial inspection of the situation to feel a positive urge to lead his singleton Diamond at the third trick. Did you instinctively decide on the Diamond lead? Chess players call a move similarly based on an immediate reaction of chess-sense to a given situation 'a positional move'.

HAND NO. 7
FLEXIBILITY

♠ 9 6 4 3
♡ A Q 10 6 3
◇ K 9
♣ A Q

♠ Q J 5
♡ J 2
◇ A J 7 5 4 2
♣ K J

You are South, and your contract is Three No-Trumps. West leads the ♣6. When you have recovered from the shock of the horrible duplication of values in Clubs, and before playing to the first trick, you have to decide

ON WHICH OF THE RED SUITS WILL YOU BASE THE PLAY OF THE HAND?

If the outstanding Hearts break 3–3 and the King is with West, you have nine certain tricks. The probability of the Hearts behaving as accommodatingly as all that is 18 per cent. If they don't, you will need a third Diamond trick. But if that suit yields a third trick, it will automatically produce others. Then why not play on Diamonds? That's right. Diamonds should have priority.

SO HOW DO YOU PLAY TO THE FIRST TRICK?

You keep the ♣K as an entry to the closed hand for the long Diamonds, and take the trick with dummy's Ace. Next, of course, you cash dummy's ♢K, on which East plays the Ten, and continue with the ♢9. East shows out, discarding a Spade.

WHAT DO YOU DO ABOUT THAT?

If you put up your ♢A and shift to Hearts, you are back again at that miserable 18 per cent chance. But if you let the ♢9 run and West takes, your chance becomes 50 per cent, as you need no longer ask anything more of Hearts than that West should have the King. So you let the ♢9 run up to West. But he declines to produce his Queen, preferring to leave dummy still on lead.

WHAT'S TO DO NOW?

Lead a small Heart to your Knave. Now it doesn't matter where the ♡K lies. If it takes the trick and Clubs are played, you win in your own hand; cash the ♢A; and run the Hearts, with your contract now depending on a Heart division not more unfavourable than 4–2, which is an 84 per cent chance. If your ♡J holds the trick, your contract is safe. You cash the ♢A, and follow with another Diamond. That way you make five Diamonds, two Clubs, and two Hearts.

This hand shows the need to be ready to change your plans with changing circumstances and to seize opportunity when it presents itself.

HAND NO. 8
TRIFLES PAY DIVIDENDS

♠ K 5 2
♡ 6 3
♢ 6 5
♣ 10 8 6 4 3 2

```
        N
   W         E
        S
```

♠ A 8
♡ A 9 4
♢ A K Q 8 4 3
♣ A 5

You are South, and your contract is Three No-Trumps. West leads the ♡Q, and East plays the King.

DO YOU TAKE THE TRICK?

Certainly not. You hold up your Ace to the third round, with East following each time, and you have then ensured your contract if it happens that the opponent with the long Hearts—probably West—has no stopper in Diamonds; for you have severed the defence's lines of communication in Hearts. But suppose West does have a Diamond stopper and two Hearts left.

IS THERE STILL A CHANCE FOR YOU TO LAND YOUR CONTRACT?

Yes, if East holds the ♢J alone.

HOW DO YOU ACT SO AS TO GIVE YOURSELF THAT CHANCE?

Cross to the table with the ♠K, and lead Diamonds. If East plays the Knave, let him have the trick; and if the Knave was a singleton, you have succeeded in shutting West out of the play, although it was he, and not East, who had the real Diamond stopper. Now you can run your remaining Diamonds.

You may perhaps think that the chance of finding East with the lone $\Diamond$J was a slender one. Actually, it constitutes 20 per cent of the various 4–1 Diamond distributions that are possible. By playing so as to profit by that chance you increased your overall prospects of success by 2·8 per cent. It is a mark of the expert that his knowledge and technique yield him just such small but frequent additional chances of success as this one.

HOLD YOUR HORSES

♠ 8 6 5 2
♡ Q J 9 7
◇ 8
♣ Q 7 4 2

```
        N
   W         E
        S
```

♠ A Q
♡ K 10 6 5
◇ A 10 3
♣ A 6 5 3

You are South, and your contract is Four Hearts. West leads the ♣J.

DO YOU COVER IN DUMMY?

To cover pays in one case only—if West has the King. But if East is void of Clubs, or if he has the King singleton or doubleton, the play of the Queen would mess you up thoroughly. So you don't cover. And now East plays the King.

WHAT DO YOU DEDUCE FROM THAT? HOW DOES IT AFFECT YOUR CHANCES OF SUCCESS?

You now know that West had four Clubs in sequence to the Knave, and that you cannot avoid losing two Clubs. The defence also has the Ace of trumps. That makes it obligatory for you to take the Spade finesse. On balance, it looks as if the chances of getting your contract are about 50 per cent.

BUT ISN'T THERE A FURTHER DANGER THAN THAT OF LOSING THE SPADE FINESSE?

There is indeed. Suppose you take the first trick with your ♣A, and play trumps. If West has the ♡A, he will put it up at once, and lead the ♣10 for East to slaughter dummy's Queen with a ruff, and now all is lost beyond repair.

IS THERE ANYTHING YOU CAN DO IN ANTICIPATION OF THE DANGER?

Yes, hold up your ♣A, and let East have the first trick with the King. If he leads Spades, you must take the finesse, and if it succeeds, lead a small trump towards dummy. If West now puts up the ♡A and plays the ♣10, you duck in dummy, and if East ruffs, you play small from your hand. In effect, East has trumped his partner's trick; and that is the reward of your wisdom in refusing to take the first trick.

If dummy's ♡Q is allowed to win at the third trick, don't continue trumps. Opponents might play the Ace and another trump, and so prevent your ruffing two Diamonds in dummy. At the fourth trick cash the ♢A, ruff a Diamond on the table, and then lead a small Club. That is the safest way to return to the closed hand, as a Spade lead might be ruffed by West with a small trump. Things have indeed changed. At the beginning you feared and took action against a Club ruff; now you play a Club yourself to guard against the possibility of a damaging ruff in another suit.

The peculiarity of this hand lies in your having to play small Clubs from the table and from your hand to the first trick. The purpose of that stratagem was to prepare a situation in which you could do the same thing again—to your advantage. The key to the solution of your problem was that you knew you had to lose two Clubs anyway.

ORDER! ORDER!

♠ A J 4
♡ A 9 7 5 3
◇ A Q 9
♣ A 8

```
        N

  W           E

        S
```

♠ 7 3
♡ 6
◇ K J 10 8 6 4
♣ K 7 4 3

You are South, and your contract is Seven Diamonds. West leads the ◇5, and East follows suit.

WHAT IS YOUR PROBLEM?

You need not lose a Club, as two can be ruffed in dummy. But there is only one way to rid yourself of the losing Spade in the closed hand, and that is to establish dummy's fifth Heart and discard a Spade on it. So, assuming that the opposing Hearts are divided 4–3, you set about doing just that.

IN WHAT PRECISE ORDER DO YOU PLAN TO MAKE YOUR THIRTEEN TRICKS?

You have to trump three Hearts and only two Clubs. The danger is that you may concentrate too much on the Hearts and play in this way: 1. Trump. 2. ♡A. 3. Heart ruff. 4. ♣A. 5. Heart ruff. 6. ♣K. 7. Club ruff. 8. Heart ruff. 9. Club ruff. But now you cannot return from the table to your own hand to draw trumps except by ruffing dummy's good fifth Heart, on which you want to throw your losing Spade. Clearly, at the critical moment you have landed yourself in the wrong hand.

WHAT HAS BEEN THE MISTAKE?

Hearts were established too early. Try ruffing Clubs sooner, and you get the correct order like this: 1. Trump. 2. ♡A. 3. Heart ruff. 4. ♣A. 5. ♣K. 6. Club ruff. 7. Heart ruff. 8. Club ruff. 9. The third Heart ruff. 10. Trump. 11. Trump. 12. ♠A. 13. The high Heart. And there you are!

IF HEARTS DO NOT BREAK 4–3 IS THERE STILL A CHANCE LEFT FOR YOU?

Yes, a slight one. If West has the long Hearts and both the King and the Queen of Spades, then he will be squeezed. At the seventh trick East will fail to follow to a Heart, showing that West originally had five Hearts. You play on as prescribed, and at the eleventh trick the play of your last trump squeezes West. If he discards his last Heart, you throw a Spade from dummy; if he discards from his King and Queen of Spades, you throw dummy's Heart, and make the last two tricks with dummy's Ace and Knave of Spades.

In this hand the timing of the play—the order of the tricks— had to be just right. And the squeeze—a very simple one—has made its debut in this collection of deals.

HAND NO. 11
CONSTRUCTIVE DEFENCE

You are West, and your cards are:
    ♠ A 5 2, ♡ 10 8, ◇ 9 8 7 4, ♣ Q 9 5 2.
You and your partner sit quietly and listen to this bidding:

South	North
1 ◇	1 ♠
2 ♣	2 ♡
3 ♣	3 ◇
3 N-T	All pass

WHAT DO YOU LEAD?

Opponents have bid all four suits. When that happens, it is generally best to lead one of dummy's suits. As North bid Spades first, his Hearts may be shorter. So you attack Hearts, leading the Ten.

North exposes dummy; and here it is, with your hand repeated:

        ♠ J 10 9 7 4
        ♡ A J 4 2
        ◇ K 10 5
        ♣ J

♠ A 5 2	N	
♡ 10 8	W	E
◇ 9 8 7 4		
♣ Q 9 5 2	S	

Your ♡10 holds the trick, dummy playing the deuce, your partner the Seven, and declarer the Three. It looks as if you've led the right suit, so you continue with the ♡8. Dummy's Ace goes up; East completes his peter with the Six; and South plays the Five. Now dummy's ♣J is led, East and South following with small cards.

WHAT IS YOUR VIEW OF THE SITUATION AS A WHOLE, AND DO YOU TAKE THE TRICK?

Your partner to all appearances has two or three established Hearts. Your chief concern is how to get him in so that he can cash them. Spades present the best—perhaps the only—prospect of creating an entry for him. As for the current trick, we suggest that you take it at once with your ♣Q. Your partner may well have the ♣10; if so, your ♣9 is a second stopper.

AND WHAT SPADE DO YOU LEAD?

The Ace. South could have the King singleton, and then your access to East's hand is achieved at once. If no honour drops from South, your best continuation is still another Spade, the Five. East may have the King or the guarded Queen. In the latter case, of course, he must not cover dummy's high Spade, but must keep his Queen in the hope that South's King will come down, and that therefore you still have another Spade to give him if you get the lead again. That happens if you win a trick with your ♣9.

Good defence, quite as much as dummy play, is steered by imaginative planning.

HAND NO. 12
BETWEEN GAME AND SLAM

♠ A Q 5
♡ 8 4
◇ A Q 4
♣ J 9 7 3 2

```
        N
    W       E
        S
```

♠ K 7 4 2
♡ A K 7
◇ J 10 6
♣ A Q 6

You are South, and your contract is Three No-Trumps. West leads the ♡Q, and East plays the Six. You have a nice lot of high cards and a pleasant-looking five-card suit. You may well be feeling that perhaps you ought to have been in a slam; and if it is a duplicate match that you are playing, you may be fearing that your opponents at the other table bid Six No-Trumps and maybe made it. You, however, are only in game.

IS THERE ANY DANGER OF YOUR NOT MAKING IT?

Yes. The Heart attack hit your weak spot. You have seven immediate winners—three Spades, two Hearts, one Diamond, and one Club. In the minor suits there are finesse possibilities, any one of which would provide you with at least one of your two missing tricks, even if the finesse fails. But you can only stop Hearts once more; so you have no time for a series of promotion plays. Obviously, you will have to be very careful.

THERE IS, HOWEVER, AN ABSOLUTELY SAFE WAY OF PLAYING. CAN YOU FIND IT?

If you try the Diamond finesse and it miscarries, you will have gained only one of your two missing tricks. That does not solve your problem. So you concentrate on the Clubs. There you have a chance for a special safety-play. Attack the situation straight away by cashing the ♣A. If both opponents follow, or if West shows out, you cross to the table with a Spade, and lead a small Club. If East wins with the King, you have established at least the two extra tricks you need. In any other case, you put in the ♣Q. It either holds the trick, and you safely establish a Diamond as your ninth trick; or West takes, and dummy's Clubs give you your contract and even a chance of making twelve tricks.

That way of handling the Club suit places East on the horns of a dilemma, if he has the dangerous holding of four or five Clubs to the King-Ten. For then he must either go up with the King and establish your Queen and Knave for you, or he has to allow you to make one of your two missing tricks without losing the lead—the gain of a tempo that is precious indeed to you as it enables you at once to set up a Diamond trick that fulfils your contract. If you take the Club finesse instead of cashing the Ace, you imperil your contract if West has the singleton King.

And now let us suppose you did bid the Small Slam in No-Trumps.

HOW DO YOU PLAY THIS TIME AGAINST WEST'S SAME LEAD OF THE ♡Q?

Last time your one idea was to play safe and guard your game contract from every distribution, however remote, that could wreck it. Now, with the slam as your objective you have to live dangerously and probe every possibility that might favour you. First, of course, you try out the Diamonds; for if the ◇K is with East, you will need all the Club tricks, but if West has the ◇K, you can handle the Club suit conservatively, as then you can afford to lose a Club. So you try your luck with the Diamond finesse. If the Queen holds, you cash the ♣A as before, and any one of four things can happen.

First, the King falls from East's hand, and you now have a fair chance of an overtrick to your slam. Second, if West drops the

King, cash the ♣Q and let East have a Club trick. When you take his inevitable Heart return, you play three rounds of Spades, finishing in the closed hand. If the opposing Spades break 3–3, you don't need to finesse Diamonds again. Third, your ♣A draws only the Four and Five from opponents. You cross to the table with a Spade, and lead a small Club in the slender psychological hope that East, holding the King-Ten-Eight, will lose patience and go up with his King. Fourth, your ♣A draws the Eight from West. Now your Club lead from dummy should be the Nine in an attempt to induce East to cover if he holds King-Ten-Five. Should he play the Five, however, probably it would be best for you to go up with your Queen, hoping to drop the Ten from West.

So much for what can happen after a successful Diamond finesse. If the finesse fails, there is nothing left that you can do but take the Heart return, cross to dummy, and finesse the ♣Q. If that succeeds, you should, generally speaking, cash the ♣A on the second round. But if West drops the ♣8 on the first round, your best chance is to go over again to dummy and lead the ♣J in the hope that West's Clubs were the doubleton Ten-Eight.

HAND NO. 13
A CALCULATED RISK

♠ A 6 5 2
♡ 9
◇ 7 4 2
♣ A Q J 9 4

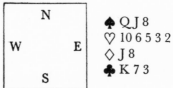

♠ Q J 8
♡ 10 6 5 3 2
◇ J 8
♣ K 7 3

You are East. The bidding:

South	North
1 ◇	2 ♣
2 N-T	3 N-T
All pass	

West leads the ♡4.

WHAT DOES THE LEAD TELL YOU ABOUT THE DISTRIBUTION OF THE SUIT, AND WHAT POSSIBILITIES CAN YOU SEE IN THE DISTRIBUTION OF ITS HONOUR CARDS?

If your partner has led his fourth highest Heart—and you have no reason to suppose that he hasn't—you know that, since you yourself have the deuce and the Three, he had four Hearts, and that the declarer has three. West may have only one honour with the Seven and Eight. Then the declarer's three Hearts are all honours, and it does not matter what card you play to the first trick. But your partner and the declarer may each have two honours, and that is the most likely and the most interesting situation. If the declarer has the Ace and either the Queen or the Knave, he can hold the suit at least twice and will generally

35

♠ A652
♡ 9
♢ 742
♣ A Q J 9 4

♠ Q J 8
♡ 10 6 5 3 2
♢ J 8
♣ K 7 3

make his contract. But if his holding is the Queen-Knave-Eight (or Seven) or the King-Knave-Eight (or Seven), then the defence has good prospects.

WHAT ARE THEY?

The defence has nine Hearts, in which you have the longer holding together with what looks like an invaluable entry card—the ♣K situated over the Ace. So Hearts may well be the suit that spells defeat for the declarer. But for that you need a second entry, and as the declarer may not have to let you make a third-round Spade trick, your only likely second entry is the ♡10. So our view is that you must not squander that possibly vital card by covering the ♡9 at the first trick. What you are hoping will happen is that you will get the lead with the ♣K, and so be able to return a Heart through the declarer's two honours to your partner's killing tenace, and that on the fourth round you will overtake West's ♡7 or ♡8 with your Ten and break the contract with your fifth Heart. Our advice, then, is that you play the ♡6 to the first trick later returning the ♡2 to tell your partner of your length and your intentions.

Admittedly, by ducking the first Heart you may be giving the declarer a trick.

IN WHICH CASES DOES THIS HAPPEN?

Generally when the declarer holds the ♡A. With the ♡A, however, he nearly always makes his contract anyway, and getting an extra trick—often only temporarily—does not essentially decide the issue. But the cases in which your duck may indeed present the declarer with a contract he could not otherwise make are when he holds the King-Queen-Eight, or King-Queen-Seven; for instance, if his Two No-Trumps rebid was a shaded one, like this:

♠ K 10 5, ♡ K Q 8, ♢ A 10 9 6 3, ♣ 10 5.

But South loses his contract even with a much stronger hand, such as

♠ K 10 5, ♡ K J 8, ♢ A K Q 10, ♣ 10 8 6,

but only if you play the way we suggest.

This is pre-eminently one of those hands on which you have to weigh various possibilities against each other, and take a view.

HAND NO. 14
A DEUCE ON GUARD

♠ 8 7 6 4 3 2
♡ 2
◇ Q J 9 2
♣ 8 4

♠ K Q
♡ A K Q J 5 3
◇ K 10 5 4
♣ 6

Both vulnerable. You are South. The bidding:

West	North	East	South
1 ♣	No	2 ♣	4 ♡
All pass			

West leads Clubs twice, and you ruff the second round. You note that the ten tricks you need are at your disposal—six Hearts, three Diamonds, and a Spade. But there is a fairly obvious danger.

WHAT IS THAT DANGER?

Opponents hold six trumps, and their most likely distribution is 4–2. So if you draw trumps right away, you will have only one left yourself when you start establishing Diamonds. The defence would take their Diamond Ace and force out your last trump with a Club. You can now cash your Diamonds all right, but when you lead a Spade, you lose to the Ace, and the play of another Club defeats you.

♠ 876432
♡ 2
♢ Q J 9 2
♣ 84

♠ K Q
♡ A K Q J 5 3
♢ K 10 5 4
♣ 6

CAN YOU AVOID THIS DANGER?

Quite easily. You lead the ♠Q at the third trick, and now the lowly little trump in dummy protects your own trumps from being shortened by a Club lead. That way of playing keeps you a tempo ahead of the defence. The lead of the ♠Q is a shade better than the ♠K because, if West has the Ace, he may duck, and then you have gained right away the one Spade trick you need, and can turn at once to clearing trumps.

BUT WHAT ABOUT STARTING ON DIAMONDS AT THE THIRD TRICK? ISN'T THAT JUST AS GOOD AS PLAYING A SPADE?

Certainly not. It is true that whether you play a Spade or a Diamond you avail yourself equally of the momentary protection dummy's trump gives you against being forced. But suppose the opponent with the ♢A decides to hold it up? You dare not lead Diamonds again—or for that matter a Spade—for fear of a Diamond ruff developing. So now you simply must draw trumps, and the original danger of a Club force remains. But with Spades, you remember, a first-round duck by West, so far from embarrassing you, is something that you actually try to induce. The crux of the matter is, of course, that you have to make three Diamond tricks but only one Spade.

THE GENTLE ART OF HOODWINKING

♠ J 8 3
♡ Q 10 8 2
♢ K J 2
♣ K Q 6

```
        ┌─────────────┐
        │      N      │
        │             │
        │  W       E  │
        │             │
        │      S      │
        └─────────────┘
```

♠ A K Q 6 4 2
♡ 9 6
♢ Q 4
♣ J 5 2

East-West vulnerable. You are South, and your contract is Four Spades. West leads the ♣4, and East takes dummy's Queen with the Ace and returns the ♣3. South plays the Five, West the Nine, and dummy's King wins.

HOW MANY TRICKS MUST YOU EXPECT TO LOSE? AND WHY DO WE SUGGEST YOU COUNT LOSERS?

The defence can make three more tricks—the ♢A and Two Hearts, and so defeat you. In suit contracts a count of losers generally reveals most realistically what you are up against. After that, you may count your winners, potential as well as actual; and that often helps you to perceive a possible way of saving a seemingly hopeless situation. Here, for instance, you can count, in addition to the Club trick you have already won, six sure trump tricks, the master ♣J, and two potential tricks in Diamonds, making in all the ten tricks you need. But for both potential Diamond tricks to become actual, opponents must obligingly refrain from cashing their two top Hearts when the lead passes to the defence with the ♢A.

♠ J 8 3
♡ Q 10 8 2
◇ K J 2
♣ K Q 6

♠ A K Q 6 4 2
♡ 9 6
◇ Q 4
♣ J 5 2

SO WHAT TACTICS DO YOU ADOPT?

You must play in such a way as to make it appear to your opponents, first, that it would be inadvisable for them to attack Hearts; and, secondly, that they have a safe or even profitable way of getting off lead. In short, your only hope is to manage to get into their minds a totally wrong picture of the hand. You have already taken the first step in that direction when you won the second trick on the table and left the question 'Who has the ♣J?' an open one for your opponents.

WHAT IS YOUR NEXT STEP?

Lead the ♠3 from dummy and play the Queen from your own hand. Now cash the ♠A. This evolution has the appearance of a trump finesse followed by an attempt to drop the ♠K with the Ace. You hope to make each of your opponents imagine that his partner holds the King of trumps.

IF ALL THE OPPOSING TRUMPS WERE DRAWN IN THE TWO ROUNDS, WHAT DO YOU DO NOW?

Lead the ◇4. Should West go up with the Ace, play low from dummy; but if the Ace does not appear, put on dummy's King. If it holds, lead dummy's ◇2, and you have a very good chance of getting a Diamond or a Club return from either opponent. For you have certainly done a good deal towards confusing the issues, and your deceptive manœuvres may well have convinced your opponents that Hearts are for them a 'don't touch me' suit which you are trying to get them to lead.

IF THE OPPOSING TRUMPS ARE NOT DIVIDED 2–2, HOW DO YOU PLAY?

Just the same as before. More than two rounds of trumps would give the defence too much scope for signalling.

HARD LUCK?

♠ 8 6 3
♡ A Q 7 5
◇ 4
♣ A J 8 6 4

♠ K J 9
♡ K J 6 3
◇ A
♣ Q 9 7 5 2

Neither vulnerable. You are South. The bidding:

South	West	North	East
1 ♣	1 ◇	3 ♣	No
3 ♡	No	4 ♡	All pass

West leads the ◇Q to your Ace, and you play two rounds of trumps, with both opponents following suit.

WHAT ARE YOUR PROSPECTS?

Your certain tricks are four Hearts, four Clubs, and a Diamond—nine tricks. As for possible tricks, you might catch the ♣K and so make five Club tricks. Then Spades might yield one or even two tricks. So there is the possibility of taking twelve tricks. But you had best put such dreams of overtricks out of your head. There is no law against East holding the ♣K and West the ♠A-Q-10. So don't wait for that to happen and for North's commiserating 'Hard luck, partner' at the end of the hand. Do

♠ 863
♡ A Q 7 5
♦ 4
♣ A J 8 6 4

something now in anticipation of the cards lying as badly as that, and ensure your contract.

♠ K J 9
♡ K J 6 3
♦ A
♣ Q 9 7 5 2

WHAT IS THE COMPLETELY SAFE WAY OF MAKING TEN TRICKS?

Play in such a way that when West gets the lead, he will have to give you your tenth trick whatever he leads. For that to happen you must first strip West of every exit card—an exit card being one that will neither win nor lose a trick when led and so would allow West to rid himself safely of the lead.

HOW DO YOU PUT THIS SOUND IDEA INTO EFFECT?

Draw the last opposing trump with the third round of Hearts, and cash the ♣A. Whatever happens, play a second round of Clubs. If East has the guarded ♣K, he gets the lead and plays a Spade. You cover at random; West takes the trick, and now has to lead. But he has only Spades and Diamonds left in his hand. If he plays Spades, he gives you a trick in that suit; if he tries Diamonds he gives you a ruff-and-discard.

WHY WOULD IT HAVE BEEN WRONG TO FINESSE CLUBS?

Because East may have the King singleton, in which case he returns a Spade and West, on taking the trick, still has a Club to exit with. Note that if East is void of Clubs, West has an exit card in his third Club when he is on lead with the ♣K on the second round of Clubs. But it avails him not at all, for you take the third round of Clubs and throw him in again with a Spade.

In this hand the evolution known as 'elimination and throw-in' makes its first appearance in these pages, though on a small scale. For the declarer's task of eliminating or stripping, which often has to be so elaborate as to involve his own and dummy's hands as well as the hand of the opponent who is to be thrown-in, is here confined to stripping West of Clubs. No elimination is necessary for the North-South hands, nor is it even possible, as they have identical suit lengths.

HAND NO. 17
HUNT THE SLIPPER

♠ K
♡ A Q
♢ A 9 7 5
♣ A 9 8 6 5 2

♠ A Q J 4
♡ K J 10 7
♢ 8
♣ Q J 10 7

You are South. The bidding:

South	West	North	East
1 ♣	4 ♢	4 N-T (Blackwood)	No
5 ♢	No	6 ♣	All pass

West leads the ♢K. East trumps dummy's Ace with the ♣3 and returns a Spade.

WHAT IS YOUR PROBLEM?

If West is void of Spades, there is no slam, whether he ruffs or not. If West follows, the slam depends on your catching the King of trumps. Mathematically you should simply play out the ♣A. But on the bidding it is quite reasonable for West to have the guarded ♣K, and then only a Club finesse can land the slam.

43

♠ K
♡ A Q
◇ A 9 7 5
♣ A 9 8 6 5 2

```
        N
   W         E
        S
```

♠ A Q J 4
♡ K J 10 7
◇ 8
♣ Q J 10 7

SO DO YOU FINESSE OR DO YOU BANG OUT THE ACE OF TRUMPS?

You do neither—yet. With plenty of high cards in the side suits, and with the information revealed by the first trick that West started with eight Diamonds, you delay playing trumps and set to work to find out exactly how West's other five cards are distributed. For if you can discover that he has two Clubs, you know you must finesse.

HOW DO YOU PLAY SO AS TO BRING WEST'S DISTRIBUTION TO LIGHT?

You take East's Spade return with your Ace. Then you cash the ♠Q and ♠J, discarding dummy's ♡A and ♡Q. Now come the ♡K and ♡J (and, if necessary, the ♡10), on which dummy throws Diamonds. Let us suppose that West follows suit twice to Spades and once to Hearts, discarding a Diamond on the third round of Spades and a Diamond on the second round of Hearts.

ARE YOU THE WISER NOW?

You know all. West's original holding is now plain. He had eight Diamonds, two Spades, one Heart—and therefore two Clubs, the King and the Four. So you finesse Clubs with 100 per cent certainty of success, and make your slam. Similarly, if West produced one Spade and three Hearts, you would know he has one Club and East the other, and you would draw both by cashing the ♣A.

DOES THE CASHING OF YOUR HIGH CARDS GIVE A PERFECT COUNT OF WEST'S HAND IN ALL CASES?

There is one exception. If West follows suit to all three rounds of Spades and then shows out on the first round of Hearts, you cannot know whether he has no more Spades and two Clubs, or whether he has one more Spade and one Club. Or he might have started with five Spades and no Clubs; but then East defeats the slam anyway with his still guarded King of trumps.

HOW DO YOU DEAL WITH THIS ONE EXCEPTION?

Directly West, having followed to three rounds of Spades, reveals his Heart void, you stop playing Hearts and ruff your ♠4 in dummy. If West has no more Spades, then he has two Clubs left. So you get back to the closed hand by ruffing a Diamond, and take the trump finesse. If West follows to Spades for the fourth time, you cash the ♣A.

A remarkable feature of this hand is that once the first trick has shown West as holding eight Diamonds, you have to assume that he also has at least one Spade and one Club, for otherwise your slam cannot be made. But if he has at least one Spade and one Club, then East must have at least four Spades and four Hearts. So you were able to conduct your investigations into West's exact distribution without any fear of East spoiling things with a ruff.

DON'T BE A ROBOT

♠ Q J 7
♡ A 3
◇ A 9 3
♣ A K J 10 5

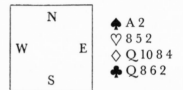

♠ A 2
♡ 8 5 2
◇ Q 10 8 4
♣ Q 8 6 2

You are East. The bidding:

North	South
1 ♣	1 ♡
3 ♣	3 N-T
All pass	

West leads the ♠3, dummy plays the Seven, and your Ace takes the trick.

DO YOU RETURN YOUR PARTNER'S LEAD, OR IS THERE ANY OTHER SUIT THAT YOU THINK WILL SERVE BETTER THAN SPADES AS A BASIS FOR THE DEFENCE?

As you yourself have the ♠2, the lead shows that your partner had only four Spades; so South has also four. But even if South's Spades are headed by nothing better than the Nine, he must make one Spade, and that may give him his ninth trick, especially as you cannot lead Spades twice. Then you must credit South who has bid the suit, with at least one trick in Hearts, such as the King or the Queen-Knave, in addition to dummy's Ace. With that kind of holding, the declarer is pretty sure to succeed in his contract provided he has also the ◇K; for then he will probably make at least one Spade, two Hearts, two Diamonds, and four Clubs. But if South lacks the ◇K, he can be defeated even if he has five ready tricks in Hearts and Spades. You realize that this analysis of the situation calls for an immediate shift to Diamonds as the most promising suit for the defence to try to exploit.

WHICH DIAMOND DO YOU LEAD?

The best shot is the ◇10. It rolls up declarer's Diamond holding even if he has the ◇J. He covers the Ten with the Knave, West covers with the King, and dummy's Ace takes. The ◇9-3 is now left on the table, waiting for West to lead through it to your tenace. Let us suppose that that is how the first round of Diamonds goes, and that dummy's ♣A and ♣K are cashed, with all following suit. Dummy's ♣J is then led.

WHAT DO YOU DO?

Take your ♣Q immediately, and return your partner's suit, Spades, hoping he has the King and can play Diamonds to you. If you duck the Club, you might find that the declarer needs only three Club tricks and gets home with five Hearts and a Diamond.

Now take the case where declarer does hold the ◇K; makes it when you lead the ◇10; and leads the ♣9 and finesses it.

AGAIN, WHAT DO YOU DO?

Take your ♣Q as before, and this time lead the ◇4. The contract can now be broken only if your partner has both the ◇J and a timely entry for leading Diamonds to you.

Automatic play would have led you astray more than once in this defence.

OTHERWISE ENGAGED

♠ 7
♡ J 7 4
◇ 8 5 3
♣ 9 7 6 5 3 2

```
        N

W               E

        S
```

♠ A K 4
♡ A K 9 6 5 2
◇ A K Q
♣ A

You are South, and your contract is Six Hearts. West leads the ♠J, and your Ace takes, East playing the ♠8.

IS YOUR CONTRACT A GOOD ONE?

It is indeed. The guiding principles for slam bidding are that the Small Slam should be bid if its chance of success is better than 50 per cent, and the Grand Slam with anything more than a 65 per cent chance. Now if you play this hand straightforwardly by simply cashing the Ace-King of trumps, your chance for twelve tricks is 90 per cent, and for thirteen tricks 53 per cent. So you are in between the prescribed limits. The 90 per cent chance for the Small Slam represents the frequency of the outstanding trumps breaking 2–2 or 3–1. Should they break 4–0, you must go down if you cash your two top trumps, losing either two trumps or one trump and a Spade.

SO CAN YOU GIVE YOURSELF A BETTER CHANCE THAN 90 PER CENT?

Any improvement can only come from a better way of handling

trumps. The standard safety-play for the nine trumps that you and dummy hold between you is to cash the Ace and, if either opponent shows out, to play small from South. But in the actual situation one of dummy's trumps is earmarked for a Spade ruff. If you cash the ♡A and lead a small trump from South, the defence, on making the Queen, might prevent the Spade ruff by playing another trump. In effect, therefore, you must regard dummy's trump holding as consisting of two trumps, not three.

WHAT, THEN, IS THE PROPER SAFETY PLAY?

Play a small Heart from South right away, and if West shows out or does not play the Queen, you put up dummy's Knave. This is a watertight way of avoiding the loss of more than one trick in the suit even if either opponent has four trumps. If it is West who has the ♡Q-10-8-3, he can only make the Queen, whether he puts it up on the first round or not. If East holds those four cards and takes dummy's Knave with the Queen, you play through him from dummy and finesse after ruffing a Spade. And neither opponent can rob you of your Spade ruff.

DOES THIS SAFETY-PLAY MAKE YOUR SLAM A 100 PER CENT CERTAINTY?

Not quite. As you cede an early trick, the defence might be able to bring off a ruff or two. Either opponent might ruff Clubs or Diamonds, or East might be able to give West a ruff in Spades. But all the distributions that make ruffs possible amount to less than 3 per cent of the frequencies. So the proper safety-play has improved your chances of making the Slam by about 7 per cent as compared with the trump-cashing method of play.

Even with as good a chance as 90 per cent in your favour, look around to see if you can find some way of bettering the percentage.

HAND NO. 20
EXPLOITING EMOTIONS

♠ 10 3
♡ A Q
◇ J 6 4
♣ A Q 8 6 5 2

```
        N
   W         E
        S
```

♠ A K 9 4
♡ J 3 2
◇ K 9 7 5
♣ 7 4

You are South, and your contract is Three No-Trumps. West leads the ♡5. East's King takes dummy's Queen, and East returns the ♡9 to dummy's Ace. West follows with the Four, and it therefore appears that he started with five Hearts.

WHAT VIEW DO YOU TAKE OF THE SITUATION?

Rather a dim one. Your only hope lies with the Club suit, which is pretty thinnish. However, you can count two Heart and two Spade tricks, so if you can manage to make five Clubs, all will be well.

HOW, THEN, SHOULD YOU HANDLE CLUBS?

You are practically defenceless against any worse distribution of the outstanding Clubs than 3–2. The position of the ♣K is also important. If it is with West and the Clubs break 3–2, you are home. But as there is no entry to dummy in the side-suits, and as opponents' holding in Clubs is worth at least one trick, it is obvious that you must let them have that trick on the first round and finesse on the second.

SO DOES IT MATTER WHETHER YOU LEAD CLUBS FROM DUMMY OR FROM THE CLOSED HAND?

As you are going to give the first Club trick away, it may seem that it does not matter. But here psychological considerations come into the picture. In bridge, as in life, there is no emotion more easy to arouse and play on than fear. If you lead a Club from your own hand and duck in dummy, that is going to upset no one. But try playing a small Club from dummy, and consider the psychological effect on East. If he has the doubleton King, he is quite likely to go up with it, fearing lest it fall to the Ace on the next round. If he has the King and two other Clubs but not the Knave, he still may feel fear of a different sort, and moreover fear reinforced by hope. For he will be hoping that his partner's five Hearts were headed by the Knave and so are now established; and he may fear that, in addition to the ♣A, you have six immediate winners in Spades and Diamonds and that you are leading to the ♣J in the closed hand to try to steal your ninth trick. Thus it could be that he will again put up his ♣K so as to get the lead and return a Heart quickly to his partner.

The mathematical chance of your taking five Club tricks is 34 per cent. But when you lead small from dummy, you make your prospects of success much rosier than that by bringing psychological factors into play.

HAND NO. 21
DEFENSIVE TIMING

♠ J 10
♡ 10 7 4
◇ K Q J 6 4
♣ A K 5

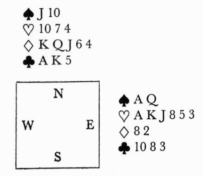

♠ A Q
♡ A K J 8 5 3
◇ 8 2
♣ 10 8 3

North-South vulnerable. You are East. The bidding:

East	South	West	North
1 ♡	1 ♠	No	3 ◇
No	3 ♣	No	4 ♠
All pass			

West leads the ♡9, you win with the King, and South plays the Queen. That does not deter you from continuing with the ♡A; there is nothing better to lead. South and West follow suit.

ON WHAT LINES SHOULD THE DEFENCE BE PLANNED?

It is likely, on the bidding, that the ◇A is with South. If so, the contract is very probably undefeatable unless the defence can make two trump tricks. But as your Queen is so badly positioned, you have to look to your partner for the second trump trick, with the promotional help of your Queen and the Heart suit of which you know both the declarer and your partner are now void. So at the third trick you again lead Hearts—the Knave, of course.

South plays the ♠9, and West a small Diamond. Declarer crosses to the table with the ♣K and leads the ♠J.

WHAT CARD DO YOU PLAY?

If your partner has only two trumps and lacks the King, the contract is unbreakable. But if he has three trumps to the Seven or better, or any four trumps, a simple device brings the declarer down. Cover dummy's ♠J with the Queen. Then, when declarer leads trumps again, your Ace makes; you lead Hearts once more; and your partner must make a trump trick if he has either of the holdings mentioned.

The essential point of your play was to decline to accept the lead until the moment when declarer was deprived of dummy's last Spade, which protected him from being over-ruffed in Hearts or shortened in trumps.

HAND NO. 22
SIMPLICITY ITSELF

♠ A J 6 3
♡ 9 7 5 2
◇ A 4
♣ A 10 3

♠ 5
♡ A Q
◇ K J 10 8 7 5 3
♣ K J 4

East-West vulnerable. You are South, and your contract is Five Diamonds. West leads the ♠K.

WHAT DO YOU THINK OF THE OUTLOOK?

Your own hand is full of holes; and as your vulnerable opponents did not bid, you have no indication of the whereabouts of their few but dangerous high cards. Clearly, what you want are leads from West, which cannot fail to be helpful.

SO WHAT PREPARATIONS DO YOU MAKE FOR THROWING THE LEAD TO WEST?

The briefest possible. Play small from dummy to the first trick and leave West with the lead. Assuming that he led the ♠K from the King-Queen, you have done all the elimination necessary by ducking; in effect, West is already thrown-in at the first trick. Whatever he leads, he must either give you a trick outright or make a finesse for you that cannot lose.

Now let us suppose that West shifts to trumps, leading a small one. You play low from dummy, and East discards a Heart.

HOW DO YOU PROCEED?

You take with your $\diamond$J; cross to the table with the Ace of trumps; ruff a small Spade in your own hand; cash the King of trumps, and lead another trump, which West has to take with his last trump, the Queen. And whatever he leads now, you make the rest of the tricks.

HAND NO. 23
DESERVING SUCCESS

♠ A J 7 5
♡ 10 3
◇ K 6 3 2
♣ K 8 4

```
        N
   W         E
        S
```

♠ K Q 10 4 2
♡ A 5
◇ A Q 4
♣ 6 5 2

You are South, and your contract is Four Spades. West leads the ♡8.

HOW MANY POSSIBLE LOSERS HAVE YOU? AND WHAT STRATEGY MUST GOVERN YOUR PLAYING OF THE HAND?

You note sadly that if North were playing the hand at Three No-Trumps, he would have nine tricks on top; while at your ten-trick contract you may lose one Heart and two or three Clubs, your Club losses depending on the position of the Ace and on which hand first plays Clubs. Clearly, your aim throughout must be to prevent West from leading Clubs through your King and to get East to lead the suit if you can.

WHAT IS YOUR FIRST MOVE TOWARDS THIS AIM?

Your first move comes now, at the first trick. You cover West's ♡8 with dummy's Ten; and when East covers, you play the ♡5 from your own hand. You covered the lead in dummy because otherwise East might not have covered; and by ducking in the closed hand you have prevented West from ever getting the lead with Hearts, and have left East on play, which is what you want.

East returns a trump, and West follows suit.

HOW DO YOU PLAY?

You take three rounds of trumps and cash the ♡A and then the Ace, the Queen, and the King of Diamonds. If both opponents follow to the three rounds of Diamonds, there is no problem.

WHAT IF WEST HAS FEWER THAN THREE DIAMONDS?

You throw the lead to East with dummy's last Diamond, discarding a Club from the closed hand. Your troubles are over, as East, whatever he leads, must give you either a Club trick or a ruff-and-discard.

BUT SUPPOSE IT IS EAST WHO IS SHORT OF DIAMONDS?

You ruff the last Diamond in your hand, and willy-nilly tackle Clubs yourself.

HOW DO YOU TACKLE CLUBS?

You lead the deuce and, whatever West plays, you put on dummy's Eight. If East wins, any return he makes gives you your contract; if West's card holds the trick and he continues the suit, you put in the King. These ways of playing the suit yield you your tenth trick:

(1) if East wins the first Club trick, either because he cannot underplay his partner's card or because West did not play a card higher than the Eight;

(2) if East has the ♣A singleton—in which case you even make an overtrick—or the Ace and one small Club; or

(3) if West has the Ace.

Should you fail despite all your craft, you have the satisfaction of knowing that this time your partner's sympathetic 'Hard luck!' is a proper epitaph.

EGGS AND BASKETS

♠ A K 10 5
♡ K 6 4 2
♢ A 8 6 4 2
♣ None

```
        N
   W         E
        S
```

♠ 7 4 3 2
♡ A J 8
♢ K Q 9 7 5 3
♣ None

You are South, and your contract is Six Diamonds. West leads the ♣A—a kindly act that gives you a ruff-and-discard right away. So now you have eleven certain tricks—six trump tricks, two Spades, two Hearts and a Club ruff.

WHAT USE DO YOU MAKE OF THE RUFF-AND-DISCARD?

The general rule is to ruff in the hand with the shorter trumps. There are exceptions, of course. For instance, preparation for cross-ruff play may require the temporary shortening of the longer trumps. Here, however, you can see no reason for departing from the rule; so you ruff in dummy, and discard from your hand. A likely-looking discard would be the ♡8, for you would then have no Heart loser. But a very little thought warns you that you would be staking everything on the outstanding Spades being favourably distributed and allowing you to make three tricks in the suit. It is true that, with the Spades distributed as they are in your two hands, there is a safety-play for making three tricks; but it is not a complete safety-play because it doesn't work against a 4–1 or 5–0 split if the singleton or void is with West. In that case you would need an alternative line of play; and as West would then have only Hearts and Clubs in his hand, clearly he could be profitably thrown-in with Hearts. But for that you would need three Hearts in your own hand; moreover, the Eight is quite high enough a card to play a valuable part in the proceedings. Therefore you decide to keep the ♡8 and discard a Spade.

You draw trumps in two rounds, and then tackle the Spades.

WHAT IS THE SAFETY-PLAY TO MAKE THREE SPADE TRICKS, ASSUMING THAT WEST HAS AT LEAST TWO SPADES?

You cash the ♠A; enter the South hand with a trump; and lead a Spade towards dummy. If West plays a small Spade, you finesse the Ten; if he plays an honour, you win with the King. No matter how the Spades lie, you make a third Spade and your contract.

HOW DO YOU PLAY IF WEST SHOWS OUT ON THE FIRST OR SECOND ROUND OF SPADES?

Now the safety-play has misfired; so you have to turn to your alternative line of play. You lead a small Heart from dummy, and just cover whatever card East puts on. If West is able to take the trick, he must either lead a Heart into your tenace or give you a ruff-and-discard by leading a Club.

It is a wise rule, at any rate at the bridge table, never to put all your eggs into one basket unless another cannot be found.

TRUMP ECONOMICS

(PLAYED BY CARL SCHNEIDER)

♠ K Q 4
♡ None
◇ J 9 4
♣ A K 9 5 4 3 2

```
      N
 W         E
      S
```

♠ A 10 7 6 5 3
♡ Q J 3
◇ A 8 2
♣ 7

You are South, and your contract is Six Spades. West leads
the ♡K.

DO YOU RUFF OR NOT?

It looks tempting to let West have the trick, discarding a Diamond
from dummy; for later on you could establish a high Heart with
a ruff, and get rid of another of dummy's Diamonds on your
winning Heart. This course would be justified if you intended to
trump your two losing Diamonds in dummy. But you cannot
afford to do that, as you need dummy's Spade honours for
drawing trumps. If West continued with the ♡A, your only
chance of making the slam would be to play for the Clubs to
break 3–2 and the Spades 2–2. You may hope for the 3–2 break,
since you are unlikely to make your contract without it. But, as
we shall see, there is no need to rely on trumps breaking evenly.
So the best play is to ruff the opening lead with dummy's ♠4.

WHAT DO YOU DO NEXT?

Cash the Ace and King of Clubs, discarding a Heart in order to prepare the way for you to ruff the suit in your own hand. Both opponents, to your great relief, follow suit to the two rounds of Clubs.

HOW DO YOU PROCEED NOW?

A third Club is led to East's Queen. Now you have a choice of three courses. First, you can let East have the trick, discarding your last Heart. East leads a Diamond, your Ace taking the trick, and you now play off dummy's King and Queen of Spades. If trumps break 2–2, you have made your slam. If not, you are down. You have played for a 40 per cent chance. Second, you can trump with the ♠10. If West over-trumps and leads the ♡A, you are down; but if the ♠10 holds, you almost certainly make your contract, having played for a 45 per cent chance. Third, you trump with the Ace; enter dummy with a Spade, both opponents following suit, and lead another Club, on which you throw your last Heart. When opponents ruff, you take the return in your hand, and cross to the table with a Spade, thus drawing the last opposing trump. Now you can run Clubs, and so land your slam. This third line of play is definitely the best, and virtually ensures your contract provided the opposing trumps are not all in one hand. It gives you—once the Clubs break 3–2— a 90 per cent chance of success. One more question. Note that we said the third way of playing 'virtually' makes the slam.

IS THERE, THEN, ANY DISTRIBUTION THAT CAN DEFEAT YOU EVEN WITH THE BLACK SUITS BREAKING FAVOURABLY?

Yes, if East has two trumps and not more than five cards in the minor suits—for example, three Diamonds and two Clubs. On the third and fourth Club leads East must throw two of his Diamonds. West must not ruff! Dummy's next lead again has to be a Club, since a trump lead runs the risk of trumps being divided 3–1. East discards his last Diamond; West trumps the trick this time, and leads a Diamond for East to ruff. But if you are unlucky enough to have that kind of distribution against you, your opponents would have to be very good players indeed to find that defence.

THE SAFE SUIT

♠ Q 4
♡ A Q 9 6 5
♢ Q 2
♣ K Q 7 4

```
        N
   W         E
        S
```

♠ A J 6 3
♡ K J 10 8 7
♢ 4
♣ 8 5 3

Both vulnerable. You are South. The bidding:

South	West	North	East
No	1 ♢	Double	2 ♢
3 ♡	No	4 ♡	All pass

West leads the ♢K and then the ♢A, which you ruff. You now draw trumps, of course—three rounds if necessary.

WHAT PRECAUTIONS DO YOU TAKE IN DRAWING TRUMPS?

The standard precautions in drawing trumps are, first, to end the process with the lead in the correct hand for the subsequent play; and, second, to unblock so as to leave at least one direct trump entry to the hand that may be going to need it. Here you want to be in your own hand when trumps have been drawn, and it is again in the South hand that you must leave at least one trump higher than trumps left in dummy.

IN THE LIGHT OF THE BIDDING, HOW DO YOU PROPOSE TO PLAY AFTER TRUMPS ARE DRAWN?

In view of East's weak raise of his partner's vulnerable opening bid, West most probably holds at least one of the two high cards still outstanding against you—the ♣A and the ♠K. If so, you ought to be able to make your contract, since either dummy's ♠Q or his King-Queen of Clubs must be favourably positioned. Your best play is to lead a small Spade towards dummy's Queen; and that was why you had to finish up the drawing of trumps in the South hand. One of three things is now likely to happen. First, if West has the King but does not put it up, you have no Spade loser. Secondly, if West does take the trick with the King, you have two discards for dummy's low Clubs on your two high Spades; and that was why you had to leave a high trump in your own hand as an entry for playing off your master Spades. Thirdly, East may have the King, and capture your Queen, in which case it is a practical certainty that the ♣A is with West.

WHY WOULD IT BE A MISTAKE TO LEAD A CLUB INSTEAD OF A SPADE WHEN YOU HAVE DRAWN TRUMPS?

Because if East has the ♣A, he could kill one of dummy's high Clubs with it, and return the suit; then when West gets the lead with the ♠K, the defence could make a Club trick and so break your contract.

We have mentioned the three most likely occurrences when you lead a Spade to dummy's Queen. Here is a fourth variation. Suppose you have to play three rounds to draw trumps, and when you lead a Spade, dummy's Queen holds the trick. You get back to the closed hand with the ♠A, both opponents following suit with small cards, and you lead a Club. West plays low, and dummy's Queen again holds the trick.

HOW DO YOU PLAY NOW?

Don't try to make an overtrick, or you may lose your contract. Lead a small Club from dummy.

We tried this hand on a number of fairly advanced players, and a remarkably high proportion of them led a Club from the South hand after drawing trumps. This suggests that it is all too easy for a bridge player to become so conditioned by the general rule of giving priority to establishing the suit that misses the Ace that he forgets to keep alert for exceptions to that useful rule.

PUTTING ON AN ACT

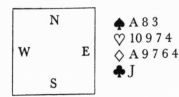

♠ 6 2
♡ K J 8
◇ K Q 10
♣ A K Q 10 5

	N		♠ A 8 3
W		E	♡ 10 9 7 4
	S		◇ A 9 7 6 4
			♣ J

Neither side vulnerable. You are East. The bidding:

North	East	South	West
1 ♣	1 ◇	1 ♡	1 ♠
2 ♡	No	4 ♡	All pass

West leads the ♠K.

WHAT PROSPECTS CAN YOU SEE OF DEFEATING THE CONTRACT?

At first sight, none. South's bidding shows he has five or six Hearts to the Ace-Queen, since clearly he has nothing much else of value. But opposite the powerful dummy that is sufficient. The declarer can lose only two Spades and one Diamond. There is no weak spot in the North-South holding.

BUT ISN'T THERE, PERHAPS, A WAY IN WHICH YOU CAN CREATE A WEAK SPOT?

Yes, there is. Or rather, there is a way in which you can create the *semblance* of a weak spot that might prove convincing enough to lead South astray. You must take over West's ♠K, cash your ◇A, and then return the ♠3. By this play you pretend to have only two Spades. West will be deceived, and, taking the trick with his Queen, will lead a third Spade. And now, if the declarer is also deceived and so ruffs with an honour in dummy, your cunning stratagem will have worked, for the high ruff will have established a trump trick for you—the setting trick.

Much will depend, of course, on whether you put on your act naturally and reasonably quickly. If you take too long to think it up, the declarer may smell a rat.

A MULTIPLE EXERCISE

♠ A K J
♡ A Q 10 8
◇ A 5 4 2
♣ A Q

```
        N
    W       E
        S
```

♠ 3 2
♡ K J 9 7 5 3
◇ K 8 3
♣ 7 4

You are South, and your contract is Six Hearts. West leads the ♡6; and we ask you also to consider the case that would arise if he led the ♠10 instead.

HOW MANY SURE TRICKS HAVE YOU? IS THE SLAM MAKEABLE?

You have eleven sure tricks—six Hearts, two Spades, two Diamonds, and one Club. Your twelfth trick may materialize from the Spade finesse, from the Club finesse, from the Diamonds being evenly divided, or from a throw-in that compels an opponent to play up to a tenace or to give you a ruff-and-discard.

WHAT, THEREFORE, MUST BE YOUR GUIDING PRINCIPLE IN PLANNING YOUR PLAY AGAINST EITHER LEAD?

To try out as many of the chances as possible, but in an order that will ensure your success if any one of them comes off. In other words, you must time your play in such a way that the failure of each attempt to land that twelfth trick will still leave you one or more chances up to the final attempt.

HOW DO YOU GIVE EFFECT TO THIS PRINCIPLE AGAINST WEST'S LEAD OF THE ♡6?

After clearing trumps and cashing the ♠A, you enter the closed hand with the ◇K and take the Spade finesse. If it succeeds, you have your slam and can even play for an overtrick. If the finesse loses and East exits with a Spade or a Diamond, you discard a Diamond on dummy's ♠K, cash his ◇A, and ruff a Diamond in your hand. If the Diamonds break 3–3, you get home by discarding a Club on dummy's fourth Diamond; and if the Diamonds fail you, you still can try the Club finesse as a last hope.

WHAT DIFFERENCE TO YOUR PLAY DOES WEST'S LEAD OF ♠10 MAKE, AND WHY?

To judge from the lead, East probably has the ♠Q. If so, you can take advantage of that circumstance—not, of course, by finessing, but by using the ♠J to throw the lead to East. So you win the first trick with the ♠K; draw trumps; cash the ◇A, the ◇K, and the ♠A; and then you lead the ♠J. When East covers, you discard your last Diamond, leaving the lead with East. If East is able to exit with a Diamond, you just have to play on in the same way as you did in the first case. But by throwing East in you have given yourself the additional chance that he may have no Diamond left. He would then have to present you with your slam by leading either a Spade, which gives you a ruff-and-discard, or a Club up to the Ace-Queen.

But suppose East doesn't play the Queen when dummy's ♠J is led, but a small Spade.

WHAT'S TO BE DONE ABOUT THAT?

You now have to consider the possibility that it may be West after all who holds the ♠Q; for the opening lead of the Ten would be correct from, say, Q-10-9-7. If you could be sure that the Queen is with West, you would naturally have to ruff dummy's ♠J to prevent West from getting the lead and returning a Club before you have tested the Diamond situation. But you cannot be sure. For if East started with some such hand as

♠ Q 8 6 4, ♡ 4 2, ◇ 10 7, ♣ K 9 6 5 2,

after two rounds of trumps, two rounds of Spades, and two

♠ A K J
♡ A Q 10 8
♢ A 5 4 2
♣ A Q

♠ 3 2
♡ K J 9 7 5 3
♢ K 8 3
♣ 7 4

rounds of Diamonds, he is reduced to black cards only. It is not very difficult for him to realize that if he plays his Queen, he may find himself well and truly thrown-in and forced to yield you your twelfth trick. So it may be that East does indeed hold the Queen, but has been wise enough to duck.

SO HOW DO YOU DECIDE WHETHER OR NOT TO RUFF DUMMY'S UNCOVERED KNAVE OF SPADES?

There is one indication that may help you to guess right, though admittedly it may be deceptive. Spades have already been round twice—the opening lead and when you crossed to the table after cashing your ♢K. Well, what cards did East play in following to those two Spade tricks? Did he play the higher Spade to the first trick? If he did, believe him. At that earliest stage of all, he could hardly have foreseen the present situation. So we suggest that you ruff the ♠J if East played normally to the first two rounds of Spades—that is, low-high—and that you discard a Diamond if he petered.

And now suppose that East was in fact wily enough to peter without having the ♠Q or a doubleton. According to plan, you refuse to ruff, discarding a Diamond; and West, to your disgust, wins with the Queen and leads a Club.

DO YOU FINESSE OR GO UP WITH THE ACE AND HOPE FOR THE DIAMOND BREAK?

A nasty question that you could answer by having a hunch and following it. But if you are to follow the counsel which the late Ely Culbertson used to speak of as coming from 'Old Man Mathematics', you will take the 50 per cent chance of the finesse; for although neither opponent showed out on the two rounds of Diamonds already played, the probability of an even division is still below 50 per cent. To round off this analysis:

CAN YOU PLAY THIS HAND IN SIX NO-TRUMPS AND MAKE THE SLAM, DOUBLE DUMMY, AGAINST A CLUB LEAD AND ANY DEFENCE AND DISTRIBUTION?

Very easily. Unless East has both the ♠Q and the ♣K, a simple finesse makes the contract. If he does have both, however well guarded, he will be thrown-in with the ♣K at the eleventh trick, and must play a Spade up to dummy's tenace.

HAND NO. 29
A FATAL DISCLOSURE

♠ 5
♡ K 6 4
◇ K Q 10 6 2
♣ A 8 6 3

```
        N
   W        E
        S
```

♠ A 9 6 2
♡ A 5 2
◇ J 9 5
♣ K 5 2

You are South, and your vulnerable opponents allowed you and your partner to bid yourselves into Three No-Trumps. West leads the ♠4, and East plays the Ten.

DO YOU TAKE WITH YOUR ACE AT ONCE?

A mere glance at the cards tells you that you are going to need the Diamond tricks that are yours once the Ace has been got out of the way. The danger, of course, is that one of the opponents—West, most likely—may have been dealt Five Spades. If so, and if you take the first trick, the defence will have easy communication in Spades, and when the lead passes to them with the ◇A, they will probably be able to run off four Spade tricks without it mattering much which opponent had the ◇A. But if you hold up the ♠A for a bit, there is a chance that communications may become difficult for the defence; for the opponent with the long Spades may not hold the ◇A. So you decide to duck a couple of rounds of Spades.

When you have played low to the first trick, East continues Spades, leading the Queen.

♠ 5
♡ K 6 4
◇ K Q 10 6 2
♣ A 8 6 3

♠ A 9 6 2
♡ A 5 2
◇ J 9 5
♣ K 5 2

DOES THAT CONVEY ANYTHING TO YOU?

It flashes the news that East has the ♠J as well. For if he had held the Queen-Ten without the Knave, he would have played the Queen to the first trick.

WHAT IMPORTANCE DO YOU ATTACH TO THAT?

The very greatest. For if, as seems to be the case, West's opening lead was from a five-card suit, the fact that East holds the ♠J suggests a play that will land your contract with complete safety.

WHAT IS THAT WINNING PLAY?

You must change your mind about ducking twice, for East's news has transformed the situation. You take the Queen with the Ace, and the suit is now blocked, no matter which opponent holds the ◇A. For if West has five Spades—which is the danger you have been fearing—East's Knave is now single. You lead Diamonds, of course; and if East has the ◇A and returns his ♠J which West overtakes, or if West has the ◇A and leads his ♠K on which East's Knave has to drop, your ♠9 will in either case become a trick.

WHAT HAPPENS IF YOU DUCK THE SECOND ROUND OF SPADES AS YOU HAD INTENDED TO DO? WHY IS IT AN INFERIOR PLAY NOW THAT EAST HAS LED THE QUEEN?

If your opponents have four Spades each, it doesn't matter how you play; they can only make three Spades and the ◇A. But if West has five Spades to the King and the ◇A, ducking a second time loses you the contract. For East leads the ♠J at the third trick. If you take it, West has two Spades to make when he gets in with the ◇A. If you duck again, West overtakes, forces out your ♠A, and makes the setting Spade trick when the ◇A gives him the lead.

And now just a word about the defence. We hope you have made a mental note that if you find yourself in East's position of having the Queen-Knave-Ten of our partner's suit, you will play the Knave to the first trick and not the Ten. By playing the Ten and then the Queen East foolishly broadcast information that solved his opponent's problem.

DANGER RIGHT AND LEFT

♠ Q J 8 6 4
♡ K 2
♢ K Q 10 7 3
♣ A

♠ 5
♡ A J 10 8 6 5 3
♢ A 8 6 4
♣ 4

Both vulnerable. You are South. The bidding:

North	East	South	West
1 ♠	5 ♣	5 ♡	Double
All pass			

West leads the ♣3, and East drops the King.

YOUR PROSPECTS? WHAT HAVE YOU TO FEAR?

There seem to be two losers—a Spade and, to judge by West's double, a Heart. The first thing to be feared is that, on the bidding, East may have all the remaining Clubs with a Spade entry, and West may have all the missing trumps. So if you cash the King and Ace of trumps and lead the ♡J, West could take with the ♡Q and give East the lead with a Spade. Then, owing to West's overruffing position, the return by East of a Club would promote West's ♡9 to a trick—the setting trick.

♠ Q J 8 6 4
♡ K 2
◇ K Q 10 7 3
♣ A

♠ 5
♡ A J 10 8 6 5 3
◇ A 8 6 4
♣ 4

CAN YOU PREVENT THIS HAPPENING?

Yes, by leading a Spade at once to cut the defence's communication in that suit. Unfortunately, this device could fail if East started with ten Clubs, two Spades, and a small Heart; for West could take your Spade lead and give his partner a Diamond ruff. East's Club return would then set up for West the trump trick that defeats you as before.

IS THERE ANY WAY OF CIRCUMVENTING BOTH DANGERS?

There is. At the second trick you lead dummy's trump deuce to your Ace. If both opponents follow, you play another trump, and your contract is safe. If East shows out, that settles the Diamond ruff danger; so now you can play a Spade to cut communications. If East takes and returns a Club, ruff in the closed hand with a small trump. Should West overruff, dummy also overruffs ruff the King. You now return to the closed hand with a Spade withand lead the ♡J. West wins, and whatever he plays gives the South hand the lead and you your contract. If West does not overruff, you cash the King of trumps, get back to your hand with a Spade ruff, and continue as before.

WOULD IT NOT BE JUST AS GOOD TO PLAY THE ♡J TO THE SECOND TRICK AND LET WEST MAKE HIS QUEEN RIGHT AWAY?

Not quite as good. For if West had originally four trumps and a singleton Diamond, he could break the contract by leading Diamonds at the third trick. You would take the Diamond and cash dummy's ♡K, but what do you do then? If you try to get back to your hand with a Diamond, West ruffs and puts East in the lead with a Spade to give him another Diamond ruff for the second undertrick. If you lead a Spade, East wins and gives West a Diamond ruff—and you are one down.

The peculiar situation in this deal called for an unusual handling of the trump suit. You had to keep the trump King in dummy to counteract West's overruffing threat on a Club lead from East.

THE GOOD AND THE BETTER

♠ K Q J 6
♡ A K Q J 10
♢ J 5 2
♣ 6

♠ A 10 5 2
♡ 7
♢ A K 6
♣ J 8 4 3 2

You are South, and your contract is Six Spades. West leads the ♡8.

WHAT IS A GOOD, STRAIGHTFORWARD WAY OF PLAYING THE HAND?

Three rounds of trumps; then reeling off Hearts, discarding three Clubs and the ♢6; next, cashing the ♢A and ♢K and ruffing a Club and a Diamond after conceding a Club. That is a natural, reasonable plan. It depends for its success, however, on drawing trumps in three rounds—a 3–2 break of the opposing trumps, which has a mathematical chance of 68 per cent.

ARE YOU GOING TO ACCEPT THAT AS THE LAST WORD ON THE HAND?

Indeed not. A moment's thought tells you there is a simple way to provide for a 4–1 break in trumps. At the second trick you draw one round of trumps with the Ace; next you cash the ♢A and ♢K; then you cross to the table with a second round of

♠ K Q J 6
♡ A K Q J 10
◇ J 5 2
♣ 6

♠ A 10 5 2
♡ 7
◇ A K 6
♣ J 8 4 3 2

Spades, thus probing the trump situation. If both opponents follow to the two rounds of trumps, you simply draw their last trump and play on as in your first plan. But if either opponent shows out on the second round of trumps, you stop drawing them. Instead you lead a Heart, discarding the last Diamond from your hand, and ruff dummy's last Diamond with the ♠ 10. Then play off all dummy's Spades and Hearts, finally conceding a Club. That plan disposes of a 4–1 trump division all right, but it fails if the Diamonds break more unfavourably than 5–2, unless the Queen drops.

IS THE SECOND PLAN, THEN, SO MUCH BETTER THAN THE FIRST?

The first plan depends on a 3–2 trump break, the second on the Diamonds being no worse than 5–2 or on the Queen being singleton. Leaving remote side-issues out of the calculation, you will find that the second plan's chance of success is about 89 per cent, compared with the first plan's 68 per cent—an improvement of 21 per cent.

And now take the case of East failing to follow to the first round of trumps.

HAVE YOU STILL A CHANCE AGAINST WEST'S FIVE TRUMPS?

Yes, if he also has five Hearts and at least two Diamonds. In this particular case it doesn't matter whether you play trumps at the third trick, as in the first plan, or cash your two high Diamonds as in the second.

The moral of this hand is: Don't let a good, sound plan that's sticking out a mile stop you from looking for a better.

HAND NO. 32
SEEK THE WEAK SPOT

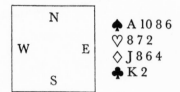

♠ K J 5 3
♡ K 10 5
◇ 10 3
♣ Q 8 4 3

```
        N
                    ♠ A 10 8 6
  W           E     ♡ 8 7 2
                    ◇ J 8 6 4
        S           ♣ K 2
```

North-South vulnerable. You are East. The bidding:

South	North
1 ♡	1 ♠
2 ◇	2 ♡
2 N-T	3 N-T
All pass	

West leads the ♣5, and dummy's Three is played.

WHICH CLUB DO YOU PLAY?

The King. Your partner may have led away from the Ace, so you had better make the matter clear to him lest the declarer, taking the trick fairly cheaply, should return the ♣J and West should put up his Ace, crashing your King. Then again, if West has led from a minor honour, your King is doomed anyway, and by playing the deuce you would allow South to make three immediate tricks in Clubs.

Your King holds the trick, South playing the Nine.

WHAT DO YOU THINK OF THE SITUATION?

Your partner's lead looked like being his fourth-high Club. That means he had a four-card suit; for you yourself have the deuce

♠ K J 5 3
♡ K 10 5
◇ 10 3
♣ Q 8 4 3

♠ A 10 8 6
♡ 8 7 2
◇ J 8 6 4
♣ K 2

and you can see the Three and the Four in dummy. South, then, had three Clubs, and his play of the Nine may have been an unblocking move. Altogether there seems small prospect of the defence getting anywhere much by continuing with the Club suit. So you count the declarer's hand. As he bid Hearts and Diamonds, he presumably has eight red cards. Add his three Clubs, and it is clear that he cannot hold more than two Spades. That suit, then, would seem to be the most vulnerable point for you to attack. So you lead Spades, praying for the Queen to be in your partner's hand.

WHICH SPADE DO YOU LEAD?

The Ten. That lead produces three tricks for you and your partner in all cases where West has Three Spades to the Queen. For your Ten would drive out dummy's Knave; and whenever West got in, the lead of his ♠Q would roll up the whole Spade suit. To lead the ♠6 or the ♠8 could turn out less favourably if South should have the Nine and the Seven. For West would cover with his Queen, and dummy's King would make; then West's Spade lead, later, would be ducked in dummy. True, you would make your Ten, but you would now need another Spade lead from your partner to obtain three tricks from the suit; and he might not get in more than once.

Suppose South's cards are something like

♠ 9 7, ♡ A Q J 7, ◇ A K Q 5, ♣ J 9 6,

and even that strong hand can be defeated in Three No-Trumps; but only by your playing in the way we recommend.

The defence in this hand and the defence in Hand No. 18 have certain features in common. Did you remember the earlier occasion and turn it to good account this time? Both hands illustrate the value, especially in defending against No-Trumps contracts, of not returning your partner's lead without first taking a careful look round in case the situation calls for a shift of suit; and both deal with ways of handling a suit in defence—a theme that is all too rarely treated adequately in text-books on play.

HAND NO. 33

A STUDY IN LYING

(PLAYED BY MICHELE GIOVINE)

♠ J 10 7
♡ A Q 8 3
◇ A 8
♣ A Q J 9

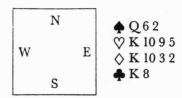

♠ Q 6 2
♡ K 10 9 5
◇ K 10 3 2
♣ K 8

East-West vulnerable. You are East. The bidding:

North	South
1 ♣	1 ♠
2 N-T	3 ♠
4 ♠	All pass

West leads the ♡2; dummy's Queen is played; you take the trick.

HOW DO YOU SIZE UP THE SITUATION?

It is pretty certain that West's lead was from three to the Knave, and it has turned out well. Against any other lead the declarer might have been able to get rid of the losing Heart in his own hand—perhaps on the Clubs. Despite this good start, you do not find the future at all hopeful. Hearts don't look like yielding another trick. Your visible assets are a likely trick in Clubs and a likely trick in Diamonds. Where is the setting trick to come from? You turn your attention to the trump situation, and reflect that the obvious scarcity of high cards in the declarer's hand makes it probable that what he does have is the Ace and King of

77

♠ J 10 7
♡ A Q 8 3
◇ A 8
♣ A Q J 9

♠ Q 6 2
♡ K 10 9 5
◇ K 10 3 2
♣ K 8

Spades, while the modest strength of his bidding rather suggests no more than five-card trump length. In these circumstances he is practically certain to finesse against the trump Queen, and you are dismally aware that the finesse will succeed.

CAN YOU THINK OF ANY WAY TO DETER HIM FROM TAKING THAT WINNING FINESSE?

There is only one way—to arouse in him suspicion that there is imminent danger of a ruff. Then he will not dare to finesse in trumps.

HOW CAN YOU GIVE HIM CONVINCING GROUNDS FOR SUCH SUSPICION?

To play Hearts or Diamonds will not impress him. Indeed, a Diamond lead would only make him hasten to take the trump finesse in order to settle the trump problem so that he can give his attention to getting rid of the third Diamond in his own hand that is probably worrying him a bit. No, the one and only play that can create the deterrent in his mind of a threatening ruff is to lead the ♣8. This play costs and risks nothing. The declarer will feel certain that West holds the ♣K and almost certain that you are waiting to ruff Clubs on the second round. So he will not finesse in trumps but in Clubs. Thus your singleton King remains as valuable as if you had kept it guarded. And you will make your Queen of trumps as well.

That is what happened in actual play when Michele Giovine put up that impudently brilliant defence.

HAND NO. 34
PASSAGE PERILOUS

♠ A K 10 6 4 2
♡ 3
◇ K 5
♣ 6 5 4 2

♠ 5
♡ K Q J 9 6 5 2
◇ 9 7
♣ K Q J

Both vulnerable. You are South. The bidding:

West	North	East	South
1 ◇	2 ♠	No	4 ♡
All pass			

West leads the ♣7, and East, after a little thought, plays the ♣8. You win with the Knave.

WHAT DO YOU MAKE OF THE FIRST TRICK?

It seems likely that West's lead was from a doubleton, and that East, having four Clubs to the Ace and no sure entry other than that Ace, cleverly ducked. You surmise that he hopes to take the second round of Clubs and give his partner a Club ruff. So you realize that you must not play trumps at once lest East's hope should materialize, and later the ◇A would break your contract.

♠ A K 10 6 4 2
♡ 3
♦ K 5
♣ 6 5 4 2

♠ 5
♡ K Q J 9 6 5 2
♦ 9 7
♣ K Q J

AS IT MIGHT BE FATAL TO PLAY TRUMPS, WHAT DO YOU DO INSTEAD?

You play two rounds of Spades, discarding a Club. Both opponents follow.

IS IT ALL RIGHT NOW TO PLAY TRUMPS?

No, highly dangerous. The ruffing danger has been replaced by the threat of an overruffing position if West has A-10-x in trumps. West would probably win the first round of trumps, and put his partner in with a Club. A Club continuation by East would then set up a trump trick for West.

AS AGAIN YOU DARE NOT LEAD TRUMPS, WHAT DO YOU DO THIS TIME?

You play a third round of Spades, discarding the last Club from your hand. It is true that if East should hold four Spades, you will have run into the dreaded overruffing position after all—in Spades instead of Clubs. It could be; but the danger in Clubs, if you lead a trump, is a certainty if West holds, as you fear, A-10-x.

Now let us suppose that West takes the third round of Spades, the suit breaking 3-3. West leads a Club; East puts on the Nine you ruff.

NOW HAS THE TIME FOR PLAYING TRUMPS ARRIVED?

Oh, no. West's Club lead was evidently a move to pave the way for the overruff. If you lead a trump, West will take at once; cash the ♦A, and lead another Diamond; and dummy will be thrown in with only black cards to lead up to West's overruffing position in either suit.

CAN YOU EVADE THIS DANGER?

You can. You play a Diamond from your hand towards dummy's King, thus keeping dummy's singleton trump as an exit card if West throws the lead to dummy.

And you lead the ♦7, not the ♦9.

WHY DO YOU GIVE THE ◇7 PREFERENCE?

Because it may well be that the situation is like this:

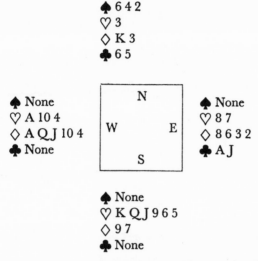

♠ 6 4 2
♡ 3
◇ K 3
♣ 6 5

♠ None
♡ A 10 4
◇ A Q J 10 4
♣ None

♠ None
♡ 8 7
◇ 8 6 3 2
♣ A J

♠ None
♡ K Q J 9 6 5
◇ 9 7
♣ None

So far you have lost one trick—the third round of Spades. If, when you lead the ◇7, West covers with the Ten, dummy's King wins; and at last trumps can safely be played, and you lose only one Heart and one Diamond, making your contract. But if you lead the ◇9 and West covers with the Ten, when dummy takes with the King and leads his trump to one of your honours, West would take his Ace of trumps, and could then lead the ◇4 for East to get the lead with his Eight. East's return of a Club would now promote West's ♡10 to the setting trick. Against the lead of the ◇7 no defence can break your contract. Of course, if West goes up with his ◇A at once, your contract is safe whatever Diamond you led. Also, if East has a higher Diamond than the Nine, it makes no difference what Diamond you lead, for you cannot prevent him from getting in. But you will know that you did what you could by being careful to keep your Nine in case East's Diamonds are headed only by the Eight.

A hand full of twists and turns, and you have had to keep wide awake to thread your way through them all and give yourself the best chances of getting home with your contract.

81

HAND NO. 35
CARD-READING AGAIN

♠ K Q 2
♡ A J 10 4
◇ Q J
♣ K 10 8 3

♠ A J 6 4 3
♡ 9 6 4
◇ 8 2
♣ A J 9

Neither vulnerable. You are South. The bidding:

South	West	North	East
No	No	1 ♣	1 ♡
2 ♠	3 ◇	3 ♠	No
4 ♠	All pass		

West leads the ◇K and continues with the ◇A. East follows first with the ◇5 and then the ◇7. West now switches to Hearts, leading the Three.

WHAT DO YOU KNOW ABOUT THAT?

Clearly East has few high cards; so it must be assumed that he bid Hearts on a five-card suit. You and dummy have seven Hearts; therefore West's ♡3 is a singleton; and you have to put on the Ace from the table to prevent East from giving his partner a ruff in the suit that would get you down straight away.

And now, of course, you play trumps, cashing first the Ace, and then crossing to the table with the King. Both opponents follow to the Ace, but East throws a Heart on the second round. Now you know a lot more about your opponents' cards.

WHAT? AND WHAT IS YOUR PROBLEM?

East's low-high play to the first two Diamond tricks indicates that West had six Diamonds; although, of course, it is just possible that East declined to peter with a doubleton Diamond, preferring to get his partner to switch to Hearts, in which case West had seven Diamonds. He had, you remember, only one Heart; and now East's lack of a second trump shows that West started with four trumps. Six Diamonds, four Spades, and one Heart add up to eleven cards. So West cannot have more than two Clubs, and East has four. Mathematically it is more probable to find the ♣Q in the larger group. Moreover, the ♣Q is the only high card in side-suits East can have to support his bid of Hearts. So you reckon East to have four Clubs to the Queen. That and West's possession of two more trumps make the handling of the Club suit rather difficult for you. In No-Trumps, for instance, with the information you now have, you would simply take two finesses, beginning with dummy's ♣10, and, if East did not cover, following up with a small Club to finesse the Knave in the closed hand. Then you would cash the ♣A, and return to the table with the ♠Q in order to play the ♣K on which East's Queen must drop. But the presence of West's trumps and his known Club shortage make that handling of the Club suit impossible.

IS THERE ANY OTHER WAY, IN THE CIRCUMSTANCES, OF EXPLOITING THE CLUB SUIT?

Yes, by means of an end-play. This must be carefully prepared. First, you unblock trumps by cashing the ♠Q. Then you lead a small Club from dummy and finesse the Knave; this, too, is an unblocking move necessary for the end-play. Next you play off your last two trumps, discarding Hearts from dummy. Now you cash the ♣A, and you have East caught in an end-play. If his last three cards are one Heart and two Clubs, you throw him in with a Heart, and he has to play from his Queen and another into dummy's Club tenace; if his cards are two Hearts and the now single ♣Q, you lead the ♣9 to dummy's King. You have to watch the fall of East's cards closely so as to judge accurately what cards he has left at the eleventh trick.

A happy ending after an unpromising start.

A SILVER LINING

♠ A Q
♡ A K 7 4 2
◇ 9 8 6 2
♣ K 4

♠ 8 6 2
♡ 5
◇ A K 10 5 3
♣ A 8 6 3

You are South, and your contract is Six Diamonds. West leads the ♣10, and dummy's King takes the trick. You cash the Ace and King of trumps, and East plays the ♠3 to the second round. So there is one certain trump loser—the Queen in West's hand.

WHAT PROSPECTS ARE THERE FOR YOUR SLAM?

Well, you can throw one of South's Spades on dummy's high Hearts, and another losing Spade on dummy's fifth Heart when it has been established by ruffing. If the Hearts break too adversely, you can still try the Spade finesse.

You begin the establishing process by cashing the Ace and the King of Hearts and ruffing a third Heart in your hand. But on the third Heart East again discards a Spade. So it has happened—the 5–2 division of Hearts.

IS THERE NOTHING FOR IT BUT TO TRY THE SPADE FINESSE?

It should not take you long to realize that although the bad news means that you cannot now ruff-out dummy's Hearts, it also means that, as West had five Hearts, you cannot be overruffed in that suit. In other words, you can now ruff Hearts with the South hand's trumps, and what is more, you can ruff Clubs with dummy's trumps—a 'Coup en passant', as it is called. You can, in short, cross-ruff with all the trumps in your two hands. And there is no need for the Spade finesse, as you now require only one Spade trick. At the thirteenth trick West, to his annoyance, may well find himself ruffing his partner's master ♠K.

BUT IS THIS CROSS-RUFF BOUND TO BRING HOME THE CONTRACT?

Not quite. If West has been dealt only one Club, you can make only seven tricks—including ruffs—in trumps, two in Hearts and one in Clubs. So in that one case you will have to depend on the Spade finesse for your twelfth trick.

WHAT, THEN, IS THE BEST WAY TO PLAY?

At the seventh trick, when you are in your own hand with the first Heart ruff, you cash the ♣A. If West doesn't ruff, your slam is safe, no matter where the ♠K lies. For the play goes: Trick 8, Club ruff; Trick 9, Heart ruff; Trick 10, a Spade, dummy's Ace winning if West doesn't ruff; Trick 11, Heart ruff; Trick 12, Club ruff. Of course, if West at any time discards a Heart, that establishes a Heart in dummy, on which you discard a Spade; and if West ruffs a Club at the eighth or twelfth trick dummy discards his ♠Q.

You rightly played a Spade at the tenth trick.

WHY WOULD IT HAVE BEEN WRONG TO PLAY ANOTHER CLUB?

It would have imperilled the slam. By ruffing the Club in dummy you would either be compelled to cash the ♠A, which West might ruff and his Heart or Club return would leave you with a losing Spade in each hand, or be compelled to ruff dummy's last Heart, leaving yourself without a trump in either hand. Then again, if West is void of Spades, he could ruff your Spade lead at the twelfth trick and make a Club trick that defeats you. That

♠ A Q
♡ A K 7 4 2
◇ 9 8 6 2
♣ K 4

♠ 8 6 2
♡ 5
◇ A K 10 5 3
♣ A 8 6 3

could happen if West originally held five Hearts, three Diamonds, and five Clubs—and you played badly.

When you were confronted with this slam, the ♣K had already been played to the first trick.

WOULD IT HAVE BEEN IMMATERIAL IF WE HAD TAKEN THE FIRST TRICK FOR YOU WITH THE ACE?

No, it would not. For if you had played for the same chances, the order of the tricks would have been: 1, ♣A; 2, ◇A; 3, ◇K; 4, ♡A; 5, ♡K; 6, Heart ruff; 7, ♣K; 8, Heart ruff; 9, South plays Spade, West discards Club, dummy's Ace takes; 10, Heart ruff; 11, Club ruff. Dummy is on play having the ♠Q and one trump. The South hand has no trump left; the contract is defeated. Of course you can avoid end-playing yourself like that by cashing the ♣K at the sixth trick instead of ruffing a Heart. Now the cross-ruff works smoothly, and you may end up with the winning position as before.

Yet there is still something unsatisfactory in that order of playing.

CAN YOU SPOT WHAT IT IS?

If West should ruff the ♣K and return a Spade, you just have to guess whether to finesse or not. But at that stage, with only two rounds of Hearts played, there are still two chances of making the twelfth trick—the finesse or ruffing-out the Hearts. That was why in the actual play you were careful not to cash the ♣A until you had had the bad news about the Heart distribution on the third round. When that was known, West's Club ruff and Spade return would not have placed you in any dilemma, since the Spade finesse would then have been your only hope.

The minutiae of analysis have not, we hope, obscured the real significance of this hand, which is that 'bad' distribution of suit-lengths in opponents' hands may often be turned to one's own advantage by a little clear thinking.

OPTIMISM HAS LIMITS

♠ K 5 4 2
♡ 5 3 2
◇ 6
♣ A 8 6 5 2

♠ A 6 3
♡ A K Q J 10 4
◇ Q
♣ K 7 3

East-West vulnerable. You are South, and your contract—believe it or not—is Six Hearts. West leads the ♠Q. It does happen, you know, once in a while that you find yourself in a thoroughly bad contract for no good reason; and this is a thoroughly bad slam, with, it would seem, at least one loser in Spades, and one in Diamonds, and maybe one in Clubs.

WHAT DO YOU DO ABOUT IT?

Well, actually, if you had it in your power to arrange your opponents' cards just as you wished, you could, with the Spade lead, so distribute them as to make your slam a certainty even if your opponents played as demi-gods. But the mathematical probability of the particular distribution happening is so extremely slight that you put that pipe-dream out of your mind for now, and look for some more likely form of optimism. There is nothing far-fetched, for instance, in your hoping for the opposing trumps and the opposing Spades to be evenly divided; and it is quite reasonable to expect the Clubs to break 3–2. None of these distributions is unusual, though you will be lucky to

87

♠ K 5 4 2
♡ 5 3 2
♢ 6
♣ A 8 6 5 2

```
      N
  W       E
      S
```

♠ A 6 3
♡ A K Q J 10 4
♢ Q
♣ K 7 3

find them all just so. If you are as lucky as that, the slam can be made. But there is a proviso—a double one.

AND THAT IS?

That you duck the first round of Spades, and that West continues the suit.

IS THERE ANY REASON FOR WEST TO BE SO OBLIGING?

Yes, there is. You note with satisfaction that East cannot follow suit with any Spade lower than the Seven, and your hope is that West will regard his partner's card as signalling encouragement. You, of course, do what you can to foster that illusion by playing the ♠6 to the trick, thus keeping your tell-tale Three from his gaze.

Let us suppose it works.

HOW DO YOU PLAY WHEN WEST LEADS SPADES AGAIN AT THE SECOND TRICK?

You take with the Ace, and draw trumps in two rounds, leaving the ♡5 in dummy. At the fifth trick you cross to the table with the ♠K, hoping for the vital 3–3 break. If that happens, you discard a small Club on the thirteenth Spade; cash the ♣K and then the ♣A; and ruff a Club in your own hand with an honour. If the Clubs are divided 3–2, you have landed your slam. All you have to do now is to return to dummy by leading your carefully preserved ♡4 to dummy's ♡5 and play a Club on which you throw your ♢Q.

Note that if the outstanding trumps do not fall in two rounds, you still have the rather slight chance of finding East with two more Spades, three Clubs, and the Ace-King of Diamonds. He can then be squeezed progressively in those three suits by your playing off all your trumps, discarding a Diamond and two Clubs from dummy.

AND NOW CAN YOU WORK OUT THE ONE KIND OF DISTRIBUTION AGAINST WHICH, WITH AN OPENING SPADE LEAD, YOU MAKE YOUR SLAM NO MATTER WHAT YOUR OPPONENTS DO?

Give East one Spade, one or two Hearts, two Clubs, and eight or nine Diamonds to the Ace-King, and you walk your slam by taking the first trick with the ♠A, cashing the Ace and King of Hearts and the Ace and King of Clubs, and throwing East in with your ♢Q at the sixth trick. Trick 7, East must return a Diamond, which you ruff in dummy, discarding a Club from your hand; Trick 8, Club ruff; Trick 9, ♡Q; Trick 10, ♠K; Trick 11, a master Club from dummy, on which you throw South's losing Spade. Nor does it help the defence if East declines to take the ♢Q. For you then draw the last trump (if East had only one and nine Diamonds), and throw West in with a Club. Whether he now leads a Diamond or a Spade you lose no more tricks, discarding your losing Spade, as before, on dummy's good Clubs.

But you were right, weren't you, to by-pass this one real chance of making your slam and to prefer as more practical the psychological chance of West being induced to continue Spades, plus the reasonable chances of favourable suit breaks.

AMBIVALENT

♠ A Q 10 4
♡ 8 6 5 3
◇ A 5
♣ J 10 8

♠ 9 7
♡ A
◇ K Q J 10 9
♣ A K Q 9 3

You are South, and your contract is Seven Clubs. West leads the ♡Q, and East plays the Seven. You have all the tricks but one at your immediate disposal—five Clubs, five Diamonds, and the Aces of Hearts and Spades.

WHERE IS THE THIRTEENTH TRICK TO COME FROM?

From the Spade finesse or from dummy reversal play that would yield you six Club tricks instead of five. The finesse is a 50 per cent chance, the dummy reversal 68 per cent.

WHICH DO YOU CHOOSE?

Neither—or, rather, both. Of course, if you must choose, you would naturally take the more probable chance—dummy reversal. But you will first want to have a good look round to see whether there is any way of playing so as to avail yourself of the finesse if it turns out that reversing the dummy won't work.

IS IT POSSIBLE TO PLAY FOR BOTH CHANCES?

It is. At the second trick you cross to the table with a trump; then if both opponents have followed suit, you ruff a Heart with an honour. You return to dummy with another trump, and if both opponents again follow, you ruff another Heart with an honour. Again you cross to the table, this time with the ♢A, in order to lead the last Heart and ruff it with South's last trump. Finally, you go back to dummy with the ♠A and draw the last opposing trump with dummy's last trump, thus completing the dummy reversal. The remaining four tricks are taken with the Diamonds in the South hand, as its last Spade was, of course, discarded on dummy's last trump.

At either the second or the fourth trick your trump leads will discover for you whether dummy reversal play is or is not going to succeed. If either opponent fails to follow to the first or the second round of trumps, you know it won't. So you then abandon it; play off all your trumps and Diamonds; and end by taking the Spade finesse.

HANDSOME IS ...

♠ A 9 8 4 3
♡ A 6 4
◇ 3 2
♣ 6 3 2

♠ K Q J 7 6
♡ 5
◇ K J 6 4
♣ A Q 9

Both vulnerable. You are South, and your contract is Four Spades after an auction in which West bid and East supported Hearts. West leads the ♠10, and East follows suit.

WHAT DO YOU THINK OF THE OUTLOOK?

You have nine of the required ten tricks in view—five trumps, the Aces of Hearts and Clubs, and two Heart ruffs. And you naturally feel that the tenaces in your minor suits ought to yield your tenth trick. Surely something will lie right!

SO WOULD IT BE A GOOD PLAN TO TRY ALL THE FINESSES ONE AFTER THE OTHER?

Yes, quite a good plan. To carry it out you will need all the entries on the table to lead towards the South hand's tenaces. So you take the first trick with the ♠A and lead a Diamond, finessing your Knave. If West wins with the Queen and returns a Heart, dummy's Ace takes and a Diamond is led on which you play your King. If West takes with the Ace and returns a Heart, you ruff with an honour; cross to the table with a trump; and lead a Club, finessing the Nine. This play gives you your tenth trick even if West holds the King, provided East has the Knave-Ten. If West, however, takes your Nine with the Knave or Ten and returns a Diamond, the table ruffs, leads a Club, and you finesse with the Queen. If West wins again, you are down.

Hard luck! Every single finesse failed. Nothing would go right. And it was a reasonably good way of playing the hand, its probability of success being just over 90 per cent. But experienced players will tell you that a very good general principle with hands containing suits that can be played straightforwardly and suits that are full of holes, is to play out the smooth-running suits and let the suits with tenaces take care of themselves.

HOW WOULD YOU FOLLOW THAT PRINCIPLE WITH THE PRESENT HAND?

You take the first trick with the ♠K; cash the ♡A; ruff a Heart with an honour; return to dummy with the ♠9; and ruff another Heart. You have now eliminated Hearts, and straightforward play is at an end, with the lead in the South hand, which has been reduced to these cards: ♠ 7, ◇ K J 6 4, ♣ A Q 9.

An unpleasant-looking state of affairs, isn't it? You must now lead away from one of your tenaces, or else go over to dummy with Spades at the cost of using up the last of your own trumps.

SO DO YOU CONCLUDE THAT THE PRINCIPLE OF PLAYING OFF THE EASY SUITS FIRST IS A FAILURE WITH THIS PARTICULAR HAND?

If you do, think again; for, actually, you have now played yourself into a sure and certain winning position. All you have to do is to play a small Diamond, which East takes. If he returns a Heart, giving you a ruff-and-discard, you throw your ♣9 and ruff in dummy. Now your tenth trick is the ruff of a Club with the last of South's trumps. East's return of a minor suit you will just cover. West takes, but he is thrown-in; whatever he leads gives you a trick and your contract. This second way of playing the hand is a 100 per cent certainty, since, on the bidding, East cannot be void of Hearts and so able to ruff them at the second trick. Anyway, that risk—if it be a risk at all—also occurred in the finessing plan of play, but a trick later.

The charm of this hand is that the best way to play it is the simple, almost automatic way. No cunning is needed. The sole difficulty is to detect the winning position beneath the ugly conglomeration of tenaces.

HAND NO. 40

LOOK FOR SNAGS

♠ K Q J 9
♡ K 9 5
◇ A J 8 4
♣ A 5

♠ None
♡ A Q J 8 2
◇ K Q 6 5 2
♣ K 4 2

East-West vulnerable. You are South, and your contract is Seven Diamonds. West leads the ◇3. Your Grand Slam appears to be on ice, since the third Club in your own hand can be ruffed in dummy. And that is just the sort of occasion for you to be on your guard, to look warily around for anything, however remote, that might crack the ice and sink your slam.

ARE THERE ANY POSSIBLE DANGERS?

Yes, two—a major danger and a minor one that needs only ordinary care to render harmless. The first is that West may have all four outstanding trumps and not more than one Club. If so, the Club ruff plan is out. The minor danger is that either opponent may have five Hearts to the Ten. As you yourself have a void in Spades, it would not be so very remarkable if your opponents, too, had quite unbalanced distributions.

CAN YOU PLAY THE HAND SO AS TO MEET THESE DANGERS?

Yes, completely safely. You cover West's ◇3 with dummy's Four. If East follows suit, the Club ruff plan remains in the picture. You draw all the trumps in three rounds, cash the Ace-King of Clubs, and ruff your third Club in dummy. Now all you have to be careful to do is to follow the standard play for retaining the two-way finesse against five Hearts to the Ten in either opponent's hand by taking the first Heart trick in the hand with two or more honours—the South hand.

But if East does not follow with a trump to the first trick, you have to play differently. You put the ◊2 from your own hand on the first trick, and lead a Spade from dummy, ruffing it with the ◊K. Now you lead the ◊5 and win in dummy as cheaply as possible. You return to your own hand by ruffing another Spade with the ◊Q, and lead your last trump, the Six, finessing in dummy if necessary. Then you draw West's last trump with the table's last and master trump, discarding South's losing Club. Now you play the ♡5 from dummy, and take the trick in your hand as before.

A rather surprising appearance, this, of dummy reversal play. It provides a good illustration of the folly of playing from dummy to the first trick before you have thought things out properly. The safe way of playing when East shows out in trumps would be ruined if you had carelessly played any trump but the Four from dummy to the first trick.

NO SNAGS TO LOOK FOR

(PLAYED BY ELY CULBERTSON)

♠ 4
♡ 6 5
◇ 7 5 4
♣ K J 9 7 6 5 3

```
      N
  W       E
      S
```

♠ A 6 2
♡ A 8 3
◇ K 9 3
♣ A Q 10 4

You are South, and you start the auction with One Club. Your opponents bid and support Spades; but your partner refuses to let them have the contract, and in the end he buys it with Five Clubs. West leads the ♠K and East plays the Seven. There is one thing, and only one thing, for you to do.

CAN YOU SEE WHAT IT IS—QUICKLY?

Even if you count the ◇K as a trick, you are obviously going to be one trick short of your contract. Ruffing in dummy gains nothing, as that is the hand with the long trumps. Plainly, there isn't any possible way for you to develop that missing trick. Only your opponents can do that for you; and they are unlikely to come to your help unless you can somehow manage to mislead them. There is only one way of doing that—by ducking to the first trick.

That is what the late Ely Culbertson did in the tournament in the World Championship in Budapest before the last World

War. Culbertson sized up the situation, and ducked to the first trick, without any delay or hesitation. At the second trick West shifted to Diamonds; East took with the Ace, and returned a Heart; Mr Culbertson's Ace took the trick, and he then reeled off all the Clubs. Is it any wonder that each opponent credited his partner with having the ♠A, and that each of them discarded all his Spades but one, carefully kept to lead to his partner's mythical Ace? So finally Mr Culbertson returned to his own hand with the ◇K, cashed the ♠A, and made his eleventh trick with his remaining small Spade.

The previous hand exemplified the danger of hasty play to the first trick; this one is held out as a masterly instance of a quick decision to try to fool opponents at the first trick when any such decision had to be practically instantaneous to be convincing. There is no inconsistency, however. The two cases are quite different. In the previous hand you held overpowering cards, and had to search for hidden perils of distribution. In the present hand you did not need to be a Culbertson to take in at a glance dummy's complete emptiness, save for seven Club tricks; and you already knew your own hand, with its two unsupported Aces and one unsupported King in side-suits. No, it was not difficult to realize your plight quickly. What did require an ingenious, experienced brain, such as a Culbertson's, was to see in a flash that concealing the ♠A by ducking might cause the defence to make a fatal slip, and was the only hope of doing so.

EVASIVE ACTION

♠ Q J 6
♡ A 6 5 2
♢ A J 5 3
♣ A 4

♠ 5
♡ J 10 9 8 7 4
♢ 8 4 2
♣ K 6 3

North-South vulnerable. You are West. The bidding:

South	West	North	East
1 ♢	1 ♡	2 ♡	2 ♠
2 N-T	No	3 ♢	No
3 N-T	No	6 ♢	6 ♠
Double	No	6 N-T	All pass

You lead the ♡J; dummy's deuce is played; East puts on the Queen; South's King wins. The declarer now cashes dummy's ♢A, East playing the Queen. Dummy's ♠6 is led, and East takes with the Ace and returns the suit, South's King winning. At the fifth trick South leads the ♣J.

DO YOU COVER?

It is evident, you reflect, that the declarer's opening bid was a light one, probably something like

♠ K x x, ♡ K x, ♢ K 10 9 7 6, ♣ Q J x.

If so, he can make two Spades, two Hearts, five Diamonds, and two Clubs—eleven tricks in all. Clearly he is going to finesse in Clubs if you do not cover; but he cannot catch your King. Moreover, if you cover and he has the ♣10 as well as the ♣Q, he makes three tricks in Clubs and his slam. So it certainly looks as if your better course is not to cover.

ARE YOU SATISFIED WITH THAT REASONING? IS THERE ANYTHING FURTHER TO BE CONSIDERED?

There is. You have yet to consider what would happen, when you do not cover, if South has only the ♣Q left and not the Ten as well. At once you realize that he would cash the ♣A, the ♠Q, and all his Diamonds, and you would be inescapably squeezed in Hearts and Clubs. The squeeze would operate automatically, without preparation and without any call on declarer's skill, for you bid Hearts and he will know you have the ♣K. Clearly, then, you decide that you must cover, and by so doing transfer the guard in Clubs to your partner's Ten, thus freeing yourself to concentrate on keeping the Hearts guarded.

BUT WHAT IF SOUTH HOLDS ALL THREE HONOURS IN CLUBS—THE QUEEN-KNAVE-TEN?

In that case he makes his slam whatever you do. If you cover, that gives him three clear tricks in Clubs; if you don't cover, the squeeze gives him the twelfth trick. So covering can do no harm; but if your partner has the ♣10 and the ♣9, covering will enable you to dodge the squeeze.

RECONNAISSANCE

♠ K 5 2
♡ A K J 7
♢ Q J
♣ 6 5 3 2

```
        N
   W         E
        S
```

♠ None
♡ 6 3
♢ K 9 8 5 4 2
♣ A K Q 10 7

East-West vulnerable. You are South, and your contract is Six Clubs. Your opponents both bid Spades in the early rounds, but that did not deter you and your partner from reaching the Small Slam. West leads the ♠4.

HOW DO YOU PLAY TO THE FIRST TRICK?

To play low from the table would leave the Spade suit in a state of tension. The disadvantage of that way of playing, however, is that if West has the Ace, the opportunity to make the King would never recur; nor would the King protect you from being forced. So, weighing one thing with another, you decide to put on the King; and to your pleasure, it holds the trick. You discard a Diamond, and draw trumps in three rounds, West throwing two Spades. Now you lead a small Diamond; West plays the Six, and East's Ace wins. You ruff the Spade return.

WHAT IS YOUR PROBLEM?

Mainly, how the Diamond suit is going to behave. If the outstanding Diamonds split 3-2, you have no problem. You already know they cannot be more unfavourably divided than 4–1. But suppose they are 4–1.

CAN YOU MAKE YOUR SLAM IF EAST HAS THREE DIAMONDS LEFT?

Not for certain. All you can do to give yourself the best chance of success is to cash dummy's ◇Q; return to your hand by ruffing a Spade with your last trump; cash the ◇K, discarding a Heart from the table; and then take the Heart finesse—a 50 per cent chance of getting home.

CAN YOU MAKE YOUR SLAM IF WEST HAS ALL THE MISSING DIAMONDS?

Quite easily. You cash your ◇K and lead the ◇9, picking up West's Ten, when he plays it, with dummy's last trump.

So you would dearly like to know which opponent, if either, holds the missing Diamonds.

CAN YOU FIND OUT IN SUCH A WAY AS TO BE ABLE TO DEAL WITH EITHER CASE?

You can—by crossing to the table with the ♡A and leading the ◇Q. If East shows out, West has the missing Diamonds. So you overtake with the ◇K and lead the ◇9 as already indicated. If East follows suit, you let the Queen run. Should West follow suit too, that means the lucky 3–2 break, and the rest of the play is easy. If West shows out, then East has two Diamonds left, and your only chance now is the Heart finesse.

The point of the hand is that, to obtain the information you wanted, East must be made to play to the second Diamond trick before West. So you had to cross to the table with the ♡A in order to lead the ◇Q from dummy. No rule or standard play was involved. You had to think it out for yourself. And incidentally a preliminary round of Hearts was the proper preparation for finessing in that suit if it should prove necessary.

HAND NO. 44
COUNT AND PARTIAL COUNT

♠ A K 10
♡ A 8
◇ J 10 8
♣ J 7 5 3 2

♠ 9 5
♡ K Q J 5 2
◇ 4 2
♣ A 9 6 4

You are South, and your contract is Four Hearts after West opened with a vulnerable bid of Three Diamonds. He wins the first two tricks with the Ace and King of Diamonds, East throwing a Spade on the second round. West continues with the ◇Q, which you ruff. You draw all the trumps in three rounds.

NOW WHERE DO YOU STAND?

You can see just seven tricks in Hearts and Spades. Therefore you need three Club tricks; and as you have already lost two tricks, that means you cannot afford to lose more than one Club. You are well aware that the standard play of the Club holding in your two hands is to cash the Ace and lead a small card towards dummy's Knave. But you are also aware that an opening Three bid generally betokens an unbalanced hand; and East, too, has shown up with a singleton. So it may well be that the normal way of playing your Club holding could prove unsuitable. You would like to know something about the distribution of opponents' Clubs.

IS THERE ANY WAY OF GETTING INFORMATION WITHOUT JEOPARDIZING ANYTHING?

There is. Cash dummy's ♠K, and watch whether West follows suit or not.

IF WEST SHOWS OUT IN SPADES, HOW DOES THAT HELP YOU IN HANDLING CLUBS?

You now have a precise count on West's hand. You know from East's singleton Diamond that West started with seven of the suit, and he followed to three rounds of Hearts. Therefore his other three cards are Clubs. That being so, your only hope now is that East's singleton Club is the King or Queen. You accordingly play out the ♣A, which happens also to be the standard play with your holding.

IF WEST FOLLOWS SUIT WITH A SPADE, WHAT DIFFERENCE DOES THAT MAKE IN YOUR HANDLING OF CLUBS?

You now know that West cannot have more than two Clubs. If he has two Clubs, you make your contract automatically. If he is void in Clubs, East has four and you must be down no matter how you play. But if West has a singleton Club, the only certain winning situation is if West's singleton is the Ten. So you lead the ♣J from dummy. If East covers, you win with the Ace and West's Ten drops. Then you return to dummy to lead another Club. If East does not cover the ♣J, you run it, hoping for the Ten to drop. The lead of the ♣J has the added psychological advantage that it may tempt East to cover from K-10-8 or Q-10-8, in which case the missing honour will drop from West's hand under the Ace. Then a second Club lead from dummy lands your contract for you.

HAND NO. 45

HE WHO HESITATES ...

♠ K J 3
♡ A J 4
◇ A 4
♣ Q 9 7 6 2

♠ 9 7 6 4
♡ 10 7
◇ Q 7 5
♣ K 10 8 4

Neither side vulnerable. You are West. The bidding:

North	South
1 ♣	1 N-T
2 N-T	3 N-T
All pass	

You lead the ♠7; dummy's Knave is played; your partner pauses to think.

WHAT DO YOU DO?

You think too—and furiously. Knowing that South's One No-Trump bid betokened a balanced hand with either four Clubs or three Clubs to one or two honours and a four-card suit elsewhere so weak that he could not bid it even at the one level, you realize at once that the play of the hand is therefore likely to turn on the Club suit, in which you have a good-looking assortment but badly positioned. So you spend the few moments of East's slight trance in sizing up the various ways in which declarer may tackle the Clubs.

East now plays the ♠8 to the first trick. The declarer puts on the Five, and then leads the ♣2 from dummy. East plays the Three, and declarer the Knave.

AND YOU?

You now know that declarer had three Clubs, probably to the Ace-Knave. Whether you take the trick or not, his natural play is to cash the Ace on the second round of the suit. Something must be done to put him off playing the natural way. He would have to play differently if you could make him think that it is your partner who holds several Clubs to the King. He might then be strongly tempted to try to catch East's King, and drop what he imagined would be your singleton Ten, by leading the ♣Q from dummy.

HOW CAN YOU SUGGEST THIS LOSING LINE OF PLAY TO THE DECLARER?

By playing your ♣8 to the first trick. You must do this without the slightest hesitation, or the declarer will not be taken in. It is quite probable that he is not at all sure of nine tricks with only four Clubs making; and if you have played at a natural pace, the chances are he will jump at what seems to be a promising opportunity to try to get five tricks from the suit by crossing to the table and leading the ♣Q. If he does do that, you will have two stoppers in the suit, and your lead of another Spade will in all likelihood kill the contract. Moreover, from the declarer's point of view it would now be very risky for him to play out his ♣A, for if East had the rest of the Clubs, East would then take two tricks in the suit. It is true that South has a safety-play at his disposal. He could cross to dummy and lead the ♣9, letting it run if East plays low and overtaking with the Ace if East shows out. But this safety-play might use up all the table's entries before the Club suit is unblocked and set up. So the probability is that he will lead dummy's Queen, and so walk right into your trap. One final argument; it costs you nothing to play the ♣8, and it may ensnare the declarer. But only, be it repeated, if you play it naturally and without apparent thought.

HAND NO. 46
FAR FROM ORDINARY
(PLAYED BY GEZA OTTLIK)

♠ A K 4
♡ 9 8
◇ 9 6 5 3 2
♣ A K 9

```
        N
   W         E
        S
```

♠ 8 6 5 2
♡ A K Q 10 4
◇ None
♣ 6 4 3 2

You are South, and your contract is Four Hearts. West leads the ◇Q, which you ruff, East playing the Eight. Nine tricks—five in trumps, two Spades, and two Clubs—are almost lay-down for you. The ordinary, straightforward way of playing the hand is to draw three rounds of trumps, hoping for a 3–3 break, and then to try for a 3–3 break in either of the black suits. If one of them obliges, and you guess which it is in time, the thirteenth card in that suit gives you your tenth trick.

WHAT DO YOU THINK OF THIS PLAN?

Not much. Rehearsing the order of play in your mind, you realize that after taking three rounds of trumps and the Ace and King of one of the black suits, with both the opponents following all the time, you will still be down if an opponent shows out on the third round of the suit; for the return of a Diamond will extract your last trump, and you will have no entry for cashing the thirteenth card of the other black suit if that should be favourably divided. So you feel you don't really fancy this ordinary way of playing that involves such hazardous guessing, with the rather thinnish mathematical chance of about 15 per cent for its success.

WELL, CAN YOU FIND A BETTER PLAN?

You reflect that if your tenth trick is not to come from an established thirteenth black card, it equally cannot come from an established Diamond, as you haven't enough trumps for that and for drawing opponents' trumps as well. So you reach the conclusion that the only other conceivable source for your tenth trick is trumps.

IN WHAT WAY CAN YOU MAKE MORE THAN FIVE TRUMP TRICKS?

By a ruff in dummy. After you have trumped the opening lead you can cash the Ace and King of a black suit, and play a third round. If the suit breaks evenly, and trumps as well, you are home. And even if the black suit breaks 4–2, you still have at that stage a 50 per cent chance of ruffing your fourth card of the suit on the table. The overall chance for the success of this way of playing is only a shade better than with the ordinary plan.

And yet all the time there is a really superior way of giving yourself a very good chance indeed of landing your contract. Geza Ottlik found it when he had to play the hand.

CAN YOU SPOT IT?

The Hungarian reached the same conclusion as you—that the tenth trick had best be looked for in the form of a sixth trump trick. But he did not ruff in dummy. He ruffed in his own hand—dummy reversal play, in fact, although the actual situation had little likeness to text-book examples of that device. But once it is pointed out, the trick—as with Columbus's egg—is quite simple. You have already ruffed the opening diamond lead. There are four Diamonds left in dummy, four entries there in the Aces and Kings of the black suits, and four trumps still in your own hand. So you cross to the table four times, and ruff all dummy's Diamonds with all your trumps. And now the Nine and Eight of trumps on the table must yield you the sixth trump trick and your tenth trick. The probability of this plan coming off is more than 70 per cent.

Here is an extreme and really rather comical emergence of dummy reversal play.

HAND NO. 47
LOOK BEFORE YOU LEAP

♠ J 10
♡ A 5 2
◇ A Q J 4
♣ A Q 6 5

♠ A Q 9 8 7 5 2
♡ K Q 3
◇ K
♣ 7 3

You are South, and your contract is Seven Spades. West leads the ♡J. A bad contract, of course—a Grand Slam with the King of trumps missing. Still, there it is; and your problem is simply and solely to catch that King. But don't exclaim, with a shrug, 'Oh, well, partner, here's for sudden death or glory!' and snatch up the first trick with the Ace, lead the ♠J, and take the finesse. That is the one thing you must not do.

WHY?

Because instead of 'sudden death or glory', with you either losing to the King in West's hand or comfortably picking it up from East, it could happen that West is void of trumps. With all four trumps in East's hand, the situation will call for trump-reducing play to save you from the ignominy of having eventually to lead trumps to East's guarded King. In the course of reducing your trumps you will have to ruff one or more of dummy's winning cards. This really quite simple manoeuvre has acquired the high-sounding title of 'the Grand Coup'. In the present case East has three trumps left, and you have to ruff often enough to reduce your trumps to the same number. That is, you must ruff three times, and to do that you must enter dummy three times; and then you will have to return to dummy yet once more in order to lead a card in the end-play through East, which is the object of the exercise. Now dummy, as dealt, had three Aces as sure entries and the ♣Q as a possible entry. But if you had made the mistake of winning the first trick with the ♡A and West showed out when you took the trump finesse, you would have had to play off the ◇A in order to get the trump-reducing business going with Diamond ruffs. You would then have realized that the table still had the Ace and Queen of Clubs as entries for the second and third ruffs, but that there was no entry left for the end-play from the table. So despite your good luck in finding the ♠K with East, you must fail to make your Grand Slam playing that way.

WHAT, THEN, IS THE CORRECT PLAY?

Anticipating the possibility of East's having all the missing trumps, you win the opening lead in your own hand. Now you have the required four entries in dummy—three Aces and the ♣Q; for if West is void of trumps, you cannot make the contract unless it is he who holds the ♣K.

ASSUMING, THEN, THAT EAST HAS ALL THE MISSING TRUMPS AND THAT THE CLUB FINESSE IS RIGHT, HOW PRECISELY DO YOU EXECUTE THE GRAND COUP?

Having taken the first trick in your own hand with the ♡K, you cross to the table with the ◇A, thus clearing the way for Diamond ruffs at the moment that you enter dummy to take the trump finesse. You now play like this: Trick 3, ♠J; Trick 4, ♠10; Trick 5, Diamond ruff; Trick 6, Club finesse; Trick 7, Diamond ruff; Trick 8, ♣A; Trick 9, Club ruff; Trick 10, ♡A; Trick 11, ◇Q. If East ruffs, you overruff and draw his last trump; if he doesn't ruff, you discard the ♡Q, and dummy's lead now has East's ♠K trapped. Note that the Club entry to dummy at the sixth trick is better than the ♡A, which would make the contract depend on East having at least three Hearts.

CAN YOU BRING OFF YOUR GRAND COUP IF EAST HAS ONLY ONE DIAMOND?

Yes, but only if he has at least four Clubs and not more than five; otherwise he could discard his Clubs or his Hearts on the Diamond ruffs, and so prevent you from getting to the table often enough.

Here is yet another hand where the play to the first trick may be decisive for victory or defeat.

STOOP TO CONQUER

♠ J 10 7 2
♡ 10 6 5 2
◇ Q 6 5 4 2
♣ None

```
        N

W               E

        S
```

♠ A Q
♡ A K J
◇ A K 8 7
♣ A K J 10

You are South, and your contract is Six No-Trumps. West leads the ◇J; East plays the Three; and you take with the Ace.

HOW MANY DIAMOND TRICKS HAVE YOU?

Five—if you can get at them. For the Ten and the Nine are still missing; and if one opponent holds them both, the Seven or Eight in the South hand blocks the suit.

IS THERE ANY WAY OF UNBLOCKING?

Yes, by establishing on the table a master card in Spades or Hearts on which the blocking Seven or Eight of Diamonds can be thrown.

HOW DO YOU SET ABOUT DOING THAT?

Obviously not by cashing the ♠A and playing the Queen. Opponents are pretty sure to duck; and then cashing the Ace and King of Hearts, in the hope of dropping the Queen, and leading the Knave if the Queen does not fall, would be a risky

♠ J 10 7 2
♡ 10 6 5 2
◇ Q 6 5 4 2
♣ None

♠ A Q
♡ A K J
◇ A K 8 7
♣ A K J 10

business indeed, with the defence still having the ♠K. So you rightly decide that the only sound way of playing is to keep your top cards intact and try to draw the enemy's fire with the lesser honours. At the second trick you cash the ♡A, just to give yourself the chance of the Queen being a singleton, and then lead the ♠Q. If the King wins, you take any return in the closed hand; cash the ♠A and the ◇K; then cross to dummy with the ◇Q, and lead the ♠J, on which you discard your blocking Diamond.

IF OPPONENTS DO NOT TAKE THE PROFFERED ♠Q, WHAT IS YOUR NEXT MOVE?

Acting on the same principle, you lead the ♡J. If opponents take the trick, the continuation is as before. If they don't, you have no need to worry any more about making five tricks in Diamonds. With two Spade tricks, three Hearts, four Diamonds, and three Clubs, you have your slam in hand, and can now try for an over-trick. You lead the ♣10, and perhaps opponents will duck that too. The over-trick could come from the drop of a missing honour or from the outstanding Diamonds being divided 1–1.

A curious hand. At the third trick you led the ♠Q, then the ♡J, and again the ♣10—three under-leads in succession in a slam contract! And, finally, it is interesting to note that you cannot cash the ♣A as you did the ♡A, for the ♣A would squeeze dummy.

HAND NO. 49
SQUEEZE STRATEGY

♠ A 6 4 2
♡ A K Q
♢ 7
♣ 8 7 5 3 2

```
┌─────────────┐
│      N      │
│ W         E │
│      S      │
└─────────────┘
```

♠ K Q 8 7 5
♡ 9
♢ A K Q 6
♣ A K Q

You are South, and your contract is Seven No-Trumps. West leads Hearts. You have twelve tricks on top.

HOW ABOUT THE THIRTEENTH TRICK?

If opponents' Spades are not divided worse that 3–1, you have more tricks than you can make; and if Clubs should break 3–2, again tricks will be tumbling over each other. Those two chances give your Grand Slam a 96 per cent probability. But suppose both suits do hold you at bay with 4–0 and 4–1 distributions. After all, your two hands have a singleton each; so it would not be very surprising to find a void and a singleton against you. You would then have to look for squeeze possibilities.

TO WHAT EXTENT DO YOU THINK YOUR FOUR SUITS LEND THEMSELVES TO SQUEEZE-PLAY?

Hearts cannot furnish a menace, but might provide a squeeze-card. There are so many Spades in the two hands that a menace could be set up in either; and if an opponent has the Spades stopped, you will know which it is as soon as you have played the first round of the suit. The second round of Clubs will reveal

113

♠ A642
♡ A K Q
◊ 7
♣ 87532

```
      N
  W       E
      S
```

♠ K Q 8 7 5
♡ 9
◊ A K Q 6
♣ A K Q

which opponent has the stopper in that suit; but a Club menace can be set up only in dummy. Diamonds might furnish a squeeze-card, but there is no way of telling which opponent stops the suit—maybe both have it protected.

SO HOW DO YOU PLAY THE HAND?

The best order is the natural order. You first test Spades, and it is naturally advisable to do so by cashing a high card from the hand with two honours—the South hand. If either opponent fails to follow suit, you try out Clubs, cashing your three honours. If Clubs, too, split adversely, you start off on squeeze-play. There are two essentially different situations to be catered for.

WHAT ARE THEY?

Either the protection of both black suits is concentrated in the hand of one opponent, or each opponent protects one of them. And you know by now which of these two situations is the actual one.

HOW DO YOU PLAY IF ONE OPPONENT STOPS BOTH BLACK SUITS?

You play three rounds of Diamonds; cross to the table with the ♠A; and cash the two remaining Hearts. Dummy's last two cards are a Spade and a Club, and the closed hand has a high Spade and a small one. The play of the table's last Heart has squeezed the opponent holding the black suits, for he has had to discard from the ♣J and Knave and a small Spade. So the last two tricks are yours.

CAN YOU ALSO WIN IF THE PROTECTION OF THE BLACK SUITS IS DIVIDED BETWEEN THE OPPOSING HANDS?

Yes. You cash the two high Spades in your own hand; enter dummy with the ♠A; and again play off the last two Hearts. Dummy's hand at that stage consists of a Spade, a Diamond, and two Clubs, while the South hand is down to its original four Diamonds. One opponent has to keep his master Spade and the other his master Club; so neither is able to keep a Diamond stopper. This particular variety of double squeeze has been called the 'Magnetic Squeeze' because it draws a card of the same suit (here Diamonds) from each opponent's hand. It works automatically. All you had to do was to keep alert in case either opponent should let go one of the missing black cards. If that happened, you would immediately cash your master in that suit before entering the South hand to make the Diamonds.

As there is nothing East or West can do to evade being squeezed, your Grand Slam can always be made with a 100 per cent certainty. That is equally the case against an opening lead of a Club or a Spade. But if West opens with a Diamond lead, the vital Diamond entry to the South hand is taken out of dummy.

HOW DO YOU PLAY IF WEST LEADS A DIAMOND?

As before, you test the distribution of Spades and Clubs. If their protection is concentrated in one opponent's hand, he can again be squeezed, since you do not need a Diamond entry to your own hand. But if the controls of the black suits are divided, you no longer have a certainty of success. Even if Diamonds are controlled by one opponent alone and the same hand holds the Clubs, no squeeze is possible for lack of Club and Diamond entries in the end-play. All you can do, then, is to play for the chance of Diamonds and Spades both being controlled by the same opponent; for, if they are, you can manage a squeeze against that particular opponent, be he East or West. If, for instance, West has the Spade protection, you make your tricks in this order: 1, ◇Q; 2, ♠Q, East shows out; 3, ♣A; 4, ♣K, West shows out; 5, ♣Q; 6, ◇K, dummy discarding a Club; 7, ◇A, dummy discarding a Club; 8, ♡A; 9, ♡K, South discarding a Spade; 10, ♡Q, South discarding a Spade; if West has the sole Diamond control, he is now squeezed. For dummy's last three cards are Ace and two small Spades, and in your own hand you have the King and a small Spade and the ◇6. The mathematical probability of the success of your Grand Slam is reduced by an opening Diamond lead to 97·5 per cent.

This hand provides useful exercise in the manipulation of squeezes by purely logical considerations.

HAND NO. 50
TWO-PRONGED

♠ K 7
♡ A K 7 3
◇ 10 6 4 2
♣ K 10 6

```
        N
    W       E
        S
```

♠ A 8 3
♡ 8 6 4 2
◇ A K Q J 9 7
♣ None

You are South, and your contract is Six Diamonds. West leads the ♣Q. It is obvious at a glance that if the opposing Hearts are split 3–2, you have nothing to worry about; all you then lose is one Heart.

WHAT'S TO BE DONE IF THE HEARTS BREAK BADLY?

As Spades are easy to eliminate from your two hands, you can meet a bad break in Hearts by throwing the lead to an opponent with a Club on which you discard a Heart. Your other losing Heart will then be got rid of in the ruff-and-discard which that opponent will be forced to give you if he is thrown-in at the right moment. But clearly this plan depends on your being able to draw trumps in two rounds; for you need one of dummy's trumps for the Spade ruff in the stripping process, and another trump must remain on the table for there to be a ruff-and-discard position.

So there are two situations for you to consider. Let us first assume that the trumps break 2–1.

HOW EXACTLY DO YOU EXECUTE THE THROW-IN?

If West has the long Hearts, you throw the lead to East—and vice versa. So you have to handle dummy's Clubs in such a way as to be able to throw in either opponent at will. This you can do if, as seems most likely, West's opening lead is from the Queen-Knave and East has the Ace. Acting on that assumption, you keep the King in dummy for throwing the lead to East, and ruff the first trick in your hand. You draw trumps in two rounds, and then play two rounds of Hearts. If both opponents follow, your slam is made; you just concede a Heart trick. But if West turns out to have four or five Hearts, you ruff dummy's ♣10; cash the ♠K and ♠A and ruff a Spade on the table. Now you lead the ♣K. East wins with the Ace, and you discard a Heart. Your last Heart is discarded on East's return, which you ruff in dummy. If it is East who has the long Hearts, you play the ♣K; East covers with the Ace; and you ruff. Again you cash the ♠K and ♠A and ruff a Spade in dummy. The lead of dummy's ♣10 now allows you to discard a Heart, and throws the lead to West, whose return gives you your ruff-and-discard.

So far, so good. And now we come to the situation that arises if an opponent shows out at the second trick on the first round of trumps.

WHAT END-PLAY DO YOU THEN PLAN FOR?

A squeeze. You note that the ♣K-10 on the table is a two-card menace against both opponents, as each must keep two Clubs in order to prevent your making a trick in the suit. So you work down to this five-card position:

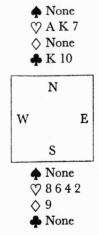

♠ None
♡ A K 7
♢ None
♣ K 10

♠ None
♡ 8 6 4 2
♢ 9
♣ None

♠ K 7
♡ A K 7 3
◇ 10 6 4 2
♣ K 10 6

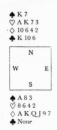

♠ A 8 3
♡ 8 6 4 2
◇ A K Q J 9 7
♣ None

knowing that as each opponent is burdened with two Clubs, neither can keep four Hearts.

Suppose, for example, that when you lead the Ace of trumps at the second trick, it is West who shows out, discarding the ♣5.

HOW EXACTLY DO YOU EXECUTE THE SQUEEZE?

Trick 3, ◇K, West discarding the ♣7; Trick 4, ♠K; Trick 5, ♠A; Trick 6, Spade ruff with dummy's ◇10, both opponents following; Trick 7, you return to your own hand with the ◇Q, West discarding a Spade; Trick 8, ◇J, West discarding a Spade, dummy a Heart, and East the ♣3. Opponents now hold between them five Hearts and five Clubs. The easy and logical order of their discards suggests a balanced Heart situation. So you cash dummy's ♡A and ♡K, and lead a Heart; and the last two tricks should be won by your ◇9 and ♡8.

It may happen that a Heart appears among opponents' discards. If so, the first round of Hearts that you play will tell you everything. If both opponents follow to Hearts, you have landed your slam. If West shows out, East is marked with four more Hearts and the singleton ♣A; so you ruff the ♣10, and the ♣K will be your winning trick. If East shows out, West has three more Hearts and the singleton ♣J; so you play out dummy's ♣K. Again, if after eight tricks the defence holds five Hearts, three Clubs, and two Spades, that shows that either the ♣A or the ♣J is by then a singleton; and you act accordingly.

A remarkable feature of this deal is that, although there are ten Clubs, including three honours, against you, dummy's three Clubs and the structure of the suit make it possible for you, as need arises, to throw-in, or to squeeze, either opponent.

HAND NO. 51
SOLO PERFORMANCE

♠ K J 7 4
♡ 6
♢ A Q 4
♣ K Q 9 7 2

♠ A Q 3 2
♡ A Q 9 4 3 2
♢ 6 3
♣ A

Both vulnerable. You are West. The bidding:

West	North	East	South
1 ♡	Double	4 ♡	4 ♠
Double	Redouble	All pass	

You naturally lead the ♡A, and the King drops from South.

WHAT DO YOU MAKE OF IT ALL?

You feel that your partner's raise to game in your suit was quite probably based on a void in Spades as well as his five Hearts to the Knave-Ten. So South probably has five trumps, and may well hold practically all the missing high cards in the minors. You therefore realize that your defence must be planned on the assumption that your partner will not be able to help in directing the play. You have to 'go it alone' and with no inkling of how the minor suits may be distributed. Your three Aces are three tricks.

WHERE IS THE SETTING TRICK TO COME FROM?

From trumps. If declarer is to lose only one trump trick, he must lead from his own hand through your collection three times. So if you force him three times—and your two black Aces ensure

119

```
        ♠ K J 7 4
        ♡ 6
        ◇ A Q 4
        ♣ K Q 9 7 2
♠ A Q 3 2     ┌─────────┐
♡ A Q 9 4 3 2 │    N    │
◇ 6 3         │ W     E │
♣ A           │    S    │
              └─────────┘
```

that you can—he will be one trump short, even
if he has five. And you gleefully perceive that
dummy's four trumps cannot protect the South
hand from being forced, because if the table is
shortened by so much as one single ruff, nothing
can prevent you from making a second trick in
trumps. So what you actually proceed to do is to give the declarer
no fewer than three ruff-and-discards.

HOW DO YOU EXPECT THE PLAY TO GO?

Your ♡A won the first trick, and you continue with Hearts,
dummy throwing a Club and South ruffing. Declarer leads a
trump, which you take with the Ace, and East shows out. Again
you lead Hearts, and South ruffs. He plays his fourth trump, and
this time you do not cover. Now comes the sixth trick, probably
a Club to your Ace. Yet again you lead Hearts, South ruffing
with his last trump. And now, whether he plays three top
Diamonds, tries Clubs, or leads a trump from the table, you
make a trump and break the contract.

At the sixth trick declarer could have led his last trump and
picked up both your remaining trumps with dummy's trump
honours. But that would have left the North-South hands without
a single trump between them; and when you got in with your
♣A, you could have run your Hearts.

MUST THIS DEFENCE OF YOURS ALWAYS PROVE SUCCESSFUL?

Indeed not. If South has five Diamonds to the King, in addition
to five trumps, he gets his contract. For, as you saw at the sixth
trick, he could strip you of all your trumps, once you have taken
your ♠A, and then run his Diamonds in peace, making three
trumps in dummy, two ruffs in his own hand, and five Diamond
tricks. There would be no need for him to let you get the lead
with your ♣A. Again, even if South has only four Diamonds, he
can get home provided they are K-J-10-9. He must realize the
situation at the outset, and take advantage of the three ruff-and-
discards you give him to get rid of the table's three Diamonds.
At the eighth trick, after South has just ruffed Hearts with his
last trump, the position is:

♠ K J
♡ None
◇ None
♣ K Q 9 7

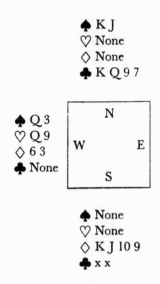

♠ Q 3
♡ Q 9
◇ 6 3
♣ None

N
W   E
S

♠ None
♡ None
◇ K J 10 9
♣ x x

South leads Diamonds, and makes the rest of the tricks. So after all your partner's cards are important, even though his rôle is a passive one. For, on the more than likely supposition from the bidding that the ◇K is with South, the success of your defence, though the best available, depends on East holding four Diamonds to at least the Nine.

Still, the hand is a pretty little duel between you and South.

VANISHING TRICK

♠ A 9 2
♡ A Q 8 7
◇ 10 5 2
♣ K Q 8

```
        N
  W           E
        S
```

♠ K 7 6 5 4 3
♡ 5 4
◇ A K Q J
♣ A

You are South, and your contract is Six Spades. West leads a Club. Obviously, the one danger is trumps.

HOW DO YOU HANDLE THEM?

You lead small from the closed hand, and if West plays the Eight you cover with dummy's Nine in case West has all four trumps and played carelessly. If that should be the situation, you would then lose only one trick in trumps; while if East wins, that is the last trick the defence can take, barring the remote possibility of an immediate ruff by West if East has, for example, six Diamonds and leads one.

But, as it happens, West is wide awake; he plays the Ten, and you win with the table's Ace. East discards a Club. The bad news is out. West still has the ♠Q-J-8 behind your King, and is smugly preening himself on the possession of two sure trump tricks.

IS THERE ANYTHING AT ALL YOU CAN DO ABOUT IT?

Yes. If the distribution of West's remaining suits should be favourable, you could end-play him with a coup that pivots your trumps and dummy's on his trumps and compels him either to surrender one of his trump tricks or else to lead from his trump tenace into your trump tenace.

HOW DO YOU PREPARE THE WAY FOR THE COUP? AND WHAT MUST WEST'S DISTRIBUTION BE FOR THE COUP TO SUCCEED?

You have to take two preparatory steps. West must be stripped of all his side-suits, and you must shorten the trumps in your own hand to two, leaving a card of a side-suit in your hand and another in dummy. All this elimination can be accomplished only if West was dealt a 4-3-3-3 hand; for otherwise he could ruff before you are ready to let him. Moreover, the number of times you must lead from dummy in order to shorten your trumps by three ruffs requires that the Heart finesse should be right.

ASSUMING THAT WEST HAS THE ♡K AND THE DESIRED DISTRIBUTION, WHAT IS THE ORDER OF PLAY TO EXECUTE THE COUP?

At the third trick you ruff a winning Club. Then you cash three Diamonds, and finesse Hearts. A second Club ruff follows. You return to dummy with the ♡A, and ruff a Heart. The position now is:

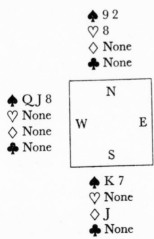

♠ 9 2
♡ 8
◇ None
♣ None

♠ Q J 8   N
♡ None
◇ None   W   E
♣ None
       S

♠ K 7
♡ None
◇ J
♣ None

You lead the ♦J, and West is caught in the trump pivot. If he ruffs with an honour, dummy's Heart is discarded, and West has to lead from his tenace; if he trumps low, dummy's ♠9 wins. So West's impressive trump holding of Q-J-10-8 has yielded him one single trick. The other trick has just disappeared.

HAND NO. 53
BATTLE OF WITS

♠ K J 9 2
♡ K 10 4
◇ 9 7 6
♣ J 10 2

♠ 6 4
♡ A Q J 9 8
◇ A K 4
♣ A K Q

Both vulnerable. You are South. The bidding:

South	North
2 ♡	2 ♠
2 N-T	3 ♡
6 ♡	All pass

West leads the ♠7. It has been a long and hard-fought rubber, with shrewd knocks given and taken by both sides. And now you and your partner have bid to a slam. You sense that West, a good player who is not afraid to take risks, is feeling chagrined and pretty desperate. Still, no good player, however desirous of making things difficult for you with an irregular lead, would ever play away from a major tenace in dummy's first-bid suit. So you refuse to place West with the Ace-Queen of Spades. It is also scarcely likely in such a position that he would lead from the Queen. But it is quite on the cards that he may be seeking to give you an awkward guess by under-leading the Ace. So you decide to bank on that view, and you put on dummy's King.

♠ K J 9 2
♡ K 10 4
◇ 9 7 6
♣ J 10 2

♠ 6 4
♡ A Q J 9 8
◇ A K 4
♣ A K Q

You are in luck. The King holds, East playing the ♠3. But you still have two losers—a Spade and a Diamond.

WHERE WILL YOU SEEK YOUR TWELFTH TRICK?

You realize that a squeeze is out of the question because when you have drawn trumps no entry will be left to the table. Your only hope is that somehow the Spade suit may yield a second trick. As dummy's Spades are still something of a tenace, you return to your own hand with a trump—both opponents following—in order to lead Spades towards dummy's holding. When you do so, West goes up with the Ace, and East plays the Five. West returns a trump, which you win on the table with the Ten, and East again follows suit. You quite justifiably feel that the appearance of West's Ace has brightened the outlook for you and presented you with real possibilities of success.

WHAT PRECISELY ARE THE WINNING POSSIBILITIES?

(1) East has the singleton ♠Q, and ruffing the Nine would make the Knave a trick.

(2) West has the singleton Ten, and leading the Knave, covered by East and ruffed in the closed hand, would make the table's Nine high.

(3) West has the singleton Queen; but that would mean he led originally from Ace-Queen-Seven, and you have already rejected that idea as incredible.

So you must choose between the first two possibilities.

HOW DO YOU DECIDE BETWEEN THEM?

Mathematics won't help you; neither position is more probable than the other. But it was rather curious, wasn't it, that West should play the ♠A on the second round. Perhaps you will be helped to a decision if you ask yourself this question:

WHY DID WEST PLAY LIKE THAT?

Either because he led originally from the doubleton Ace—which is indeed not a winning possibility for you—or because not putting up the Ace would have given the show away. If that was his reason, it means his original Spade holding was Ace-Ten-Seven. Had he played the Ten, dummy's Knave would have been captured by East's Queen; and that would have forced you to try ruffing dummy's deuce in an attempt to bring down West's Ace, for there would have been nothing else for you to try. And of course it would have worked. West is too good a player to simplify your task like that. So he put up his Ace, and gave you a guess. Fortunately, you have been able to reason your way to what is probably the winning play. You lead dummy's ♠J; ruff when East covers with the Queen; and West's Ten should drop.

A delicate little tussle, this, and centred on one suit.

INSURANCE

♠ A K J 9
♡ A Q 5
◇ J 10 2
♣ K 8 3

```
        ┌─────────────┐
        │      N      │
        │             │
        │ W         E │
        │             │
        │      S      │
        └─────────────┘
```

♠ 7 6 3
♡ K 10 2
◇ A K 8 4 3
♣ A Q

You are South, and your contract is Six No-Trumps. West leads the ♡6.

IS THE SLAM THERE ALL RIGHT?

It certainly looks like it. You have ten tricks on top, and surely two more can be obtained from Diamonds, if they are properly handled.

HOW DO YOU MAKE SURE OF FOUR DIAMOND TRICKS?

You lead a small Diamond from your hand, and unless West plays the Queen, you put on the table's Ten. If both opponents follow suit, your troubles are over. If East does not follow, you have to repeat the procedure; if West has shown out, East makes his Queen, but you pick up his Nine by finessing.

Having decided how you are going to handle the Diamonds, you now play to the first trick.

DOES IT MATTER IN WHICH HAND YOU TAKE THE LEAD?

Yes, it does—or, rather, it could. As the play of the Diamonds is all that you are concerned about, and as you have to tackle the suit by leading from the South hand, the natural thing to do would be to take the first trick in that hand and play a small Diamond at once. You are, indeed, quite likely to make your slam that way. But there is one distribution of opponents' cards that would give them an opportunity to put up a killing defence.

WHAT DISTRIBUTION AND WHAT DEFENCE?

West's ♡6 has all the appearance of being a lead from the Knave. But if it isn't; if East has some Hearts to the Knave and West has all the missing Diamonds, the play of a low Heart from dummy to the first trick will imperil your slam. For East will play the Knave. You win with the King and lead the ◇3. West ducks; dummy's Ten makes; East shows out; and you return to your hand with a Club to lead another small Diamond. This time West takes his Queen, and returns a Club, thus knocking out the South hand's last Club. Now you cannot make the table's ◇J and get back to your hand to cash the ◇A and ◇K, for you no longer have an entry outside Diamonds.

So, clearly, you decide to take the first trick in dummy.

DOES THAT ENSURE THE SLAM AGAINST THE ONE AWKWARD DISTRIBUTION?

It does—completely. At the second trick you enter your hand with the ♣A and lead the ◇3. West ducks, and the table's Ten makes as East shows out. You get back to your hand with the ♣Q and lead anothr small Diamond, which West's Queen wins. Any return he makes is won in dummy; the ◇J can now be made, as you are able to return to your hand with the ♡K in order to cash your two top Diamonds; and dummy, having thrown Spades on your two winning Diamonds, is now high.

At first sight of the North-South cards who would have thought there could be any difficulty about communications?

HAND NO. 55
A TELL-TALE SUIT

♠ Q 2
♡ A 8 5 2
◇ K Q 10 9
♣ A 5 2

```
        +-------------+
        |      N      |
        |             |
        |  W       E  |
        |             |
        |      S      |
        +-------------+
```

♠ A K 10 4
♡ 7 6 4 3
◇ A J 5 4 3
♣ None

North-South vulnerable. You are South. The bidding:

South	West	North	East
1 ◇	6 ♣	6 ◇	Double
All pass			

West leads the ♣K; dummy's deuce is played; East discards the ♠3.

WHAT ARE YOUR IMMEDIATE REACTIONS TO THE SITUATION?

The first two points to register with you are that West bid Clubs on ten of them, and that East's double seems most probably to have been based on a trick in Hearts and a stopper in Spades. Next you observe that the North-South hands readily lend themselves to dummy reversal play, thus increasing your five obvious trump tricks to six. Three top Spades and the table's two Aces bring your certain tricks to eleven. As for the twelfth trick, that could come from finessing against the ♠J or from squeezing East in the major suits. At the moment you don't much fancy having to choose between squeeze and finesse. For if West controls Hearts, East cannot be squeezed; while if West has the doubleton ♠J, the finesse, which you have to take on the second round of the suit, would fail.

At this point in your analysis you should perceive that there is a way of finding out which of the alternatives will work, and that therefore your slam can be made with complete certainty.

WHAT IS THE 100 PER CENT WINNING PLAY?

You first clear the ground by doing your reverse dummy stuff. That is, you ruff the opening lead with an honour; cross to the table with a trump; ruff the second small Club with your remaining honour; return to the table with a trump, and then cash dummy's last two trumps, discarding a Heart. You watched, of course, what trumps, if any, West had. And now you make the crucial play. It is the lead of a small Heart from dummy. You have to lose one trick, and this is the moment to concede it in order to complete your count of the three cards West was dealt outside his ten Clubs.

East probably wins the Heart trick and returns the suit to the table's Ace. Now you know all you need about West's vital three cards.

HOW DO YOU CONTINUE IF WEST ORIGINALLY HAD AT LEAST TWO RED CARDS?

In that case he cannot have more than one Spade. You cash dummy's ♣A—discarding a Heart—and his ♠Q; and then you take the Spade finesse against the Knave that East is marked with.

HOW DO YOU CONTINUE IF WEST ORIGINALLY HAD ONLY ONE RED CARD OR NONE?

You cash the ♣A, and East is squeezed. He must either throw away his master Heart or reduce his Spades to three.

If East, after taking his Heart trick, returns a Spade, you win on the table; cash the ♡A and ♣A; and East is again squeezed.

An inordinately long suit in one opponent's hand can generally be turned into a mirror in which his partner's cards are clearly reflected.

THE WORST MAY NOT BE SO BAD

♠ K 6 4
♡ 7 4 3 2
♢ 10 6
♣ A 5 3 2

```
        N
W               E
        S
```

♠ A J 8 7 5 2
♡ A K 5
♢ A K Q
♣ 4

You are South, and your contract is Six Spades. West leads the ♢9.

WHAT DO YOU THINK OF THE CONTRACT?

Not a very pleasing slam. Its fulfilment seems to depend on your not losing a trump trick, as you must certainly lose a Heart. So you make your slam if the outstanding trumps are divided 2–2 and you play off the Ace and King; if East has three to the Queen and you finesse on the second round; or if the Queen is singleton. With nine cards of the suit, the play of the Ace and King to drop the Queen is mathematically not more than about 2 per cent better than the finesse; and some players believe in finessing if there is a singleton in sight (the idea being that opponents are then likely to have a singleton, too) and in otherwise playing for the drop. All this, of course, is conditional upon there being nothing to guide you either in the bidding or in the fall of the cards up to the time when you have to make your choice. Here you do happen to have a singleton—in Clubs. So it is up to you to make your guess in whatever way you think fit, and no blame is yours if you go down.

But actually you may not have to decide. The ♠Q may fall on the first round, or one of your opponents may be void of trumps.

DOES A 4–0 SPLIT IN TRUMPS SINK ALL YOUR HOPES?

Not at all. It is true you cannot escape losing a trick to the opponent with all the trumps; but it has now become possible for you, with favouring distribution, to make the loss of that trick coincide with the playing of your Heart loser, thus coalescing the two losses into one and the same trick and so reducing them to one loss—a kind of 'loser on loser' business. You do this in an end-play that compels your trump-laden opponent to ruff your losing Heart. Moreover, he will then have to lead away from his trump tenace.

HOW DO YOU PREPARE THE WAY FOR THIS END-PLAY?

You have to strip your opponent's hand down to three trumps and your own hand to two trumps and the Heart loser. To do that you must ruff Clubs three times. Fortunately there are three entries on the table—the ♣A, the ♠K, and a Diamond ruff. But as Clubs are the suit you are going to ruff in the trump-reducing play, the Club entry has to be used before you try out the trump situation by cashing dummy's King, or you would find yourself short of an entry to the table. So your preparation must start at the second trick in anticipation of the possibility of a 4–0 trump break.

WHAT, THEN, IS THE CORRECT WAY TO PLAY THE HAND?

Having taken the opening lead with your ◇Q, you cross to dummy with the ♣A and ruff a Club. It is not till now, the fourth trick, that you lead a trump to the table's King. If both opponents follow suit, you lead trumps again; and if the Queen does not appear, you make your decision whether to finesse or play to drop the Queen. But if at the fourth trick either opponent fails

♠ K 6 4
♡ 7 4 3 2
◇ 10 6
♣ A 5 3 2

♠ A J 8 7 5 2
♡ A K 5
◇ A K Q
♣ 4

to follow to trumps, you set about completing the end-play like this: Trick 5, Club ruff; Trick 6, ◇A; Trick 7, ◇K ruffed in dummy; Trick 8, ruff of dummy's last Club; Trick 9, ♡A; Trick 10, ♡K. If there has been no ruff by the defence to spoil things, your slam is now safe; for the last three cards held by one of your opponents are trumps. You lead your ♡5; he must ruff and play a trump to your Ace-Knave. Thus it has turned out that your slam is a certainty if either of your opponents was dealt four Spades, two Hearts, three Diamonds, and four Clubs.

Rather queer, don't you think, that if West has three trumps to the Queen, the slam cannot possibly be made ; but if he has four trumps to the Queen the contract is by no means a hopeless one.

SENSATIONAL

♠ A Q 5 3
♡ J 4 3
◇ A 10 8 7 4 3
♣ None

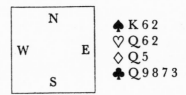

♠ K 6 2
♡ Q 6 2
◇ Q 5
♣ Q 9 8 7 3

North-South vulnerable. You are East. The bidding:

North	East	South	West
1 ◇	No	1 ♡	1 ♠
No	2 ♠	3 ♣	No
3 ♡	No	4 ♡	All pass

West leads the ♡A and continues Hearts. Dummy plays low; so do you; South wins with the Ten. He leads the ◇2; West plays the Nine; dummy's Ten covers.

WHAT DO YOU IMAGINE SOUTH'S CARDS LOOK LIKE?

He is practically certain still to be holding three Hearts to the King; his Clubs are probably five to the Ace; and he cannot have more than one Spade, for the miserable Spades that your partner bid on surely cannot be fewer than five.

HOW DO YOU THINK THE DECLARER PROPOSES TO MAKE HIS CONTRACT?

It seems pretty obvious that he intends to set up dummy's Diamonds. He is letting this round go; but he will play the Ace on the second round and ruff the third round.

♠ A Q 5 3
♡ J 4 3
♢ A 10 8 7 4 3
♣ None

♠ K 6 2
♡ Q 6 2
♢ Q 5
♣ Q 9 8 7 3

IS THERE ANY WAY YOU CAN THROW A SPANNER INTO THE WORKS?

When dummy's Diamonds have been ruffed good, the declarer will have to get back to the table to cash them. You notice with satisfaction that a Club ruff won't help him much, as you would still have a trump with which to ruff Diamonds. The declarer must draw your last trump—and dummy's in the process. So the only real entry to the table is the ♠A; and consequently the only way to upset declarer's plan of action is for you to take the first Diamond trick and lead a Spade to rob dummy of its one sure entry.

WHICH SPADE DO YOU LEAD?

Generally in leading up to a major tenace it would make little difference, as you are going to give a trick away in any case. But it suddenly strikes you—or maybe slowly dawns on you—that in the present case it is possible that South's singleton Spade might be the Knave. If so, a small Spade led by you would be won in the South hand. Declarer would then find a Club ruff useful; for it would enable him to cash the ♠A and lead another Spade in order to make the ♠Q a master by ruffing your King. He would then draw your trump with ♡K; cross to the table with the ♢A; and cash the ♠Q. In that way he would make three Spades, four trumps, a Club ruff, and the Aces of Diamonds and Clubs— just his ten tricks. But you, of course, prevent all that by simply leading your ♠K. If South has the Knave, it drops; and he can only make two Spades. And as he now has no entry in dummy, except the abortive Club ruff, he must go down on his contract unless he holds the King as well as the Ace of Clubs. This is not so very likely, as your partner must have had a few high cards outside Spades to justify—or even excuse—his bid. But even if South does hold the Ace-King of Clubs, in which case the contract cannot be broken, your play of the ♠K yields the best results for the defence.

That move of yours was a spectacular one, but it was the outcome of coldly realistic reasoning.

HAND NO. 58
ACTION BY PROXY

♠ 5
♡ K Q 9 4 2
◇ A Q J
♣ 7 5 3 2

♠ A K Q J 10
♡ 6 5
◇ 6 4
♣ A K 6 4

Neither vulnerable. You are South. The bidding:

North	East	South	West
1 ♡	4 ◇	4 ♠	All pass

West leads the ♡3; dummy's Queen is played; East takes the trick with the Ace and returns a small Diamond, which West ruffs. He leads the ♣Q; East plays the Nine; and your King wins. You draw two rounds of trumps, both opponents following.

WHAT INFORMATION HAVE YOU ACQUIRED? AND WHAT IS YOUR NEXT MOVE?

You know East was dealt eight Diamonds. As for his other cards, he has so far played two Spades, a Heart, and a Club. That accounts for twelve of his cards; his thirteenth may be a Spade, a Heart, or a Club. You realize that you've got to find which it is. For if it's a Club, West has only two left, in which case you make your contract quite simply by playing Ace and another Club.

♠ 5
♡ K Q 9 4 2
◇ A Q J
♣ 7 5 3 2

♠ A K Q J 10
♡ 6 5
◇ 6 4
♣ A K 6 4

But if East's hidden card is a Spade or a Heart, then West has three Clubs, and you will have to play to squeeze him in Hearts and Clubs. Before you can do that you must concede a trick in order to 'rectify the count'; for at present you are two tricks short of your contract, and for a squeeze to work you must be only one trick short. But this is clearly not the moment to lose a trick; more information is what you want just now. So you lead a third round of trumps.

West follows, but East throws a Diamond. So his hidden card is a Heart or a Club.

HOW DO YOU FIND OUT WHICH IT IS?

You play another Spade. This draws West's last trump, but you get no information from East—only a Diamond. So now you make your final reconnaissance by leading a Heart to dummy's King.

HOW DO YOU PLAY IF EAST DISCARDS ANOTHER DIAMOND?

As he has no Hearts, he must have a Club. Then West has only two, and your play of Ace and another Club gives you your tenth trick.

HOW DO YOU PLAY IF EAST FOLLOWS TO HEARTS?

You now have to squeeze West; and, remembering that means you must first concede a trick, you return to the closed hand with a Heart ruff in order to take the Diamond finesse, which you know must lose. East wins with his King, and his unavoidable Diamond return squeezes his partner for you. For the table's last two cards are a Heart and a Club; the South hand has Ace and a small Club; and West has been compelled either to throw away his master Heart or unguard his ♣J.

Another instance of how a really long suit held by an opponent generally enables you to pin-point the defence's distribution. But this hand also exemplifies how it occasionally happens—and it's well worth looking out for—that you can make use of the long suit by turning it against your other opponent with deadly effect.

HAND NO. 59
ICONOCLASTIC

♠ K
♡ A 10 5 4 3 2
◇ A K
♣ J 6 3 2

♠ A J 10 5
♡ J 9 8 7 6
◇ None
♣ A Q 7 4

Neither side vulnerable. You are South. The bidding:

South	West	North	East
1 ♡	Double	Redouble	2 ◇
No	No	4 N-T (Blackwood)	No
5 ♡	No	6 ♡	All pass

West leads the ♡K, taken by the table's Ace, East discarding a Diamond. You have eleven certain tricks.

HOW DO YOU PROPOSE TO SECURE THE TWELFTH TRICK?

You rightly feel that in addition to the ♡Q, West must have at least the ♣K and the Queen of Spades, if his double was at all respectable. So you plan to throw him in with his Queen of trumps at a moment when his return will give you your missing trick.

A tempting way of executing that entirely sound plan of yours is to cash the ♠K and then the Ace and King of Diamonds, discarding two Clubs from your hand. Now a trump throws

♠ K
♡ A 10 5 4 3 2
◇ A K
♣ J 6 3 2

♠ A J 10 5
♡ J 9 8 7 6
◇ None
♣ A Q 7 4

West the lead, and compels him to return a black suit; for it will be obvious to him that a Diamond return would enable you to get rid of the last losing Club in your hand, the Queen. But that way of playing is not water-tight.

WHAT'S WRONG WITH IT?

It seems unlikely from the bidding that East has five Spades, as then he would probably have preferred the major suit even to longer Diamonds. West, too, might be expected to bid Spades on five instead of doubling. So it may well be that the outstanding Spades are divided 4–4; and, if so, that makes them a more or less neutral suit. So when you throw West the lead, it is quite possible that he will lead a small Spade from his remaining Queen-to-three, and then nothing can stop him from making his ♣K.

IS THERE A BETTER WAY OF CARRYING OUT YOUR PLAN?

The throw-in was premature. Clearly, Spades as well as Diamonds must first be eliminated from your two hands; and, of course, two Clubs must be got rid of either from dummy or from the South hand to prevent West from getting off lead safely with a small Club if he has the King doubly guarded. That 'either-or' gives you the clue. As you are going to eliminate Spades, it is dummy's Clubs that you will discard on them. And there's only one way you can get into your own hand often enough to eliminate Spades—by ruffing the table's Diamonds. That they happen to be the Ace and the King is neither here nor there. You play your tricks in this order: 1, ♡A; 2, ♠K; 3, ◇A ruffed in the South hand; 4, ♠A, dummy discarding a Club; 5, ♠J, West covering and dummy ruffing; 6, ◇K ruffed; 7, ♠10, dummy discarding a Club. All is now prepared, and you lead a trump to West's Queen. Thus thrown-in, he has to return either a Club to your Ace-Queen, or a Diamond that you ruff in the closed hand while reducing dummy's Clubs to a singleton.

The right way to play the hand would have jumped to the eye if dummy had been dealt small Diamonds instead of the two highest, so enticingly apt for discarding losing Clubs on. Moral: don't let high cards hypnotize you into a false veneration if they happen to be irrelevant to the hand.

SUDDEN DEATH: SLOW FUNERAL

You are West, and South deals you this fine hand: ♠ 7, ♡ K Q 10, ◇ A K 7 5, ♣ K Q 9 6 2.

South bids Six Spades, and all pass—you with inward reluctance. You lead the ◇K, and here are your cards again and dummy's.

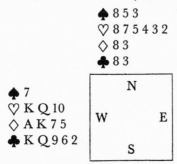

```
              ♠ 8 5 3
              ♡ 8 7 5 4 3 2
              ◇ 8 3
              ♣ 8 3
                        N
 ♠ 7
 ♡ K Q 10          W          E
 ◇ A K 7 5
 ♣ K Q 9 6 2             S
```

Your partner plays the ◇Q on your lead, and South the Four. You are relieved to observe that the declarer cannot have more than nine trumps. Moreover, your wealth of high cards in the side-suits tells you that the South hand must have at least one more loser somewhere; and in view of the Yarborough on the table, you justifiably feel that the declarer may be unable to make his slam whatever you now lead. That is quite possibly so, but it is just as well to put this question to yourself:

ARE THERE ANY THIRTEEN CARDS SOUTH COULD HAVE WHICH WOULD ENABLE HIM TO MAKE HIS SLAM?

Put that way, it should not take you too long to work out that there is one distribution, and one only, that could give South his contract. Suppose you continued with Diamonds and South's thirteen cards were: ♠ A K Q J 10 9 6 4 2, ♡ A, ◇ 4, ♣ A 4, he would ruff with an honour; cash the ♡A; lead the ♠6 to dummy's Eight; ruff a Heart with an honour; lead the ♠4 to dummy's Five; ruff a second Heart with an honour. Dummy's Hearts would now be set up, and South would lead his deuce of trumps to the table's Three to make his twelfth trick with a Heart.

So there is a possibility—just one—of the slam being made.

♠ 853
♡ 875432
◇ 83
♣ 83

♠ 7
♡ K Q 10
◇ A K 7 5
♣ K Q 9 6 2

```
        N
    W       E
        S
```

CAN YOU DO ANYTHING ABOUT IT?

Most certainly. When you mentally rehearsed the way South could establish dummy's Hearts, you noted that he had to play out the ♡A before entering dummy with the ♠8. Whether you continue with Diamonds or switch to Clubs, he can still play that way; and if you switch to Hearts, you're playing that way for him. But if you lead your trump; you alter the vital order of declarer's winning play. A trump trick has been played before the cashing of the ♡A, and now declarer is one entry short on the table. He can set up Hearts, but he cannot get at them to cash one.

So at the second trick you have theoretically broken the contract with the trump lead, no matter what South holds. But in practice, of course, he will play out all his nine trumps in the hope of you or your partner making a slip in discarding. You have still to go through that drawn-out proceeding. Let us give South the hand you imagined for him.

WHAT PRINCIPLE WILL YOU FOLLOW IN MAKING YOUR DISCARDS?

In all such situations you endeavour to discard in such a way as to help your partner to count each suit and read the declarer's hand. Your partner should be doing the same for you. In the present case, by playing the Queen to the first trick East took over protection of the Diamonds. So your first discards are the ◇A, the Seven, and the Five. East will then know that declarer has no more Diamonds, and will discard the rest of his Diamonds, so that soon you, too, will know South's Diamond was a singleton. Next you discard the King and then the Two of Clubs, telling East of your strength. He can now throw his Clubs away and cling to his three Hearts headed by the Knave. So when South leads his last Spade at the tenth trick and you have to discard from King-Queen of Hearts and King-Queen of Clubs, you throw the ♡Q, trusting to the fact that your partner has not parted with a Heart and to the argument that he would hardly have kept them so carefully if they were headed only by the Nine. He would have been more likely to discard them to give you a count of the suit.

NO OTHER WAY

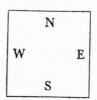

♠ A Q 5
♡ K 7 2
◇ K 9 3 2
♣ 7 6 3

♠ K 7 4
♡ J 10 4
◇ 8
♣ A Q J 9 4 2

You are West. South opened the bidding with One Diamond, and you bid two Clubs. North and South then went on to bid game in Diamonds. Your partner said No bid throughout. You lead the ♡J, which South takes with the Ace. He draws trumps in three rounds, producing the ◇A and ◇Q from his own hand and your partner following with the ◇5, ◇10, and ◇J. The declarer then makes the ♡Q from his own hand; takes the Spade finesse in dummy; cashes the ♡K, throwing a Spade from the South hand; cashes the ♠A; and ruffs a spade in the South hand. Now, at the tenth trick, he leads the ♣5. Your last four cards are Ace-Queen-Knave and a small Club. Dummy has the Nine of trumps and his three original Clubs.

WHAT IS THE DISTRIBUTION OF THE OTHER TWO HANDS?

South discarded on Hearts and ruffed a Spade; so he has nothing left in those two suits. He has one trump left; therefore his other three cards must be three Clubs, from which he has now led the ♣5. The North-South hands are thus identical in distribution. Your partner, of course, has the residue of the suits; and as you started with six Clubs and North and South have three each, East was dealt a singleton Club. His three other cards are a Spade and two Hearts.

```
      ♠ A Q 5
      ♡ K 7 2
      ◇ K 9 3 2
      ♣ 7 6 3
            ┌─────────┐
♠ K 7 4     │    N    │
♡ J 10 4    │ W     E │
◇ 8         │    S    │
♣ A Q J 9 4 2 └─────────┘
```

CAN YOU BREAK THE CONTRACT IF SOUTH HAS LED FROM THE ♣K?

Quite impossible. If you win the first Club trick, you have to return the suit to South, and his King must make; if your partner wins the trick, he has to play a Heart or a Spade and give the declarer a ruff-and-discard.

CAN YOU BREAK THE CONTRACT IF EAST HAS THE ♣K?

Yes, but only by putting up your Ace straight away and deliberately crashing your partner's King. Then you make two more Club tricks. The point is that East must not be allowed to make the ♣K, if he has it, because he cannot return you the suit, and anything else he leads would give the declarer his winning trick. Your play of the Ace at once can do no harm, and is the only hope you have of defeating the contract.

In the last hand you, as defender, robbed the declarer of his only real chance of success at the second trick; here you take your only chance at the tenth trick by carefully watching the fall of the cards and so getting a complete count of the two unseen hands.

HAND NO. 62
ENOUGH IS ENOUGH

♠ K J 8
♡ K 10 9 3
◇ K 5
♣ Q 6 4 2

```
        N
    W       E
        S
```

♠ 10 9 5
♡ A Q J 7 4
◇ Q
♣ A 10 5 3

North-South have 30 points in the first game. You are South. The bidding:

West	North	East	South
1 ◇	No	1 ♠	2 ♡
No	3 ♡	4 ◇	4 ♡
All pass			

West leads the ◇A, East playing the Knave. West switches to the ♠A, on which East plays the Six. West continues with ♠7, and you naturally win with the table's King. You draw trumps in two rounds.

WHAT DO YOU KNOW? AND WHAT IS YOUR PROBLEM?

The bidding and play have given you a fair inkling of how the East-West hands are distributed. East probably started with five Spades to the Queen, five (or four) Diamonds to the Knave,

♠ K J 8
♡ K 10 9 3
♢ K 5
♣ Q 6 4 2

♠ 10 9 5
♡ A Q J 7 4
♢ Q
♣ A 10 5 3

singleton (or doubleton) Club, and two trumps. So West was dealt five (or six) Diamonds to the Ace, four (or three) Clubs, and doubletons in the major suits. In addition to the two Aces he has played, West must be credited with the ♣K as part of his opening strength. As you have already lost two tricks, your problem is how to avoid losing more than one Club trick against the defence's holding of K-J-9-8-7 in the suit, with four of those cards probably in West's hand.

IN WHAT LINE OF PLAY WILL YOU SEEK A SOLUTION?

Clearly, you must either get West to lead Clubs to you or somehow rid one of your two hands of a losing Club. That, you reflect, is tantamount to saying that the answer lies in some kind of throw-in play.

IS THERE ANY ELIMINATION TO BE DONE TO PREPARE THE WAY FOR THROW-IN PLAY?

Yes, the ♢K must be cashed, or either opponent would have an easy way of getting off lead. On the ♢K you throw the last Spade from your own hand.

And there you stop. The temptation to complete the stripping of dummy's hand by ruffing the ♠J must be resisted.

WHY WOULD IT BE A MISTAKE TO RUFF THE ♠J?

Because it would be overdoing things; for you would then have no card with which to throw the lead to East, if that proves necessary. As for West, you have already completed the elimination process against him, as you know he has no more Spades.

SO HOW DO YOU PLAY AFTER CASHING THE ♢K?

You tackle Clubs at once, leading a small one to your Ace and returning a small one towards the table's Queen. If West wins at once with the King, all is well; he must present you with your contract either by leading a Club or by giving you a ruff-and-discard in Diamonds. But if West has four Clubs and ducks the second round, dummy's Queen wins; and now if there were no ♠J left in dummy, you would have to lead Clubs from the table and West would make two tricks in the suit. But as you have been careful to keep dummy's ♠J, you simply lead it; East covers with the Queen; you discard a Club from your own hand; and East, thus thrown-in, must give you a ruff-and-discard that enables you to get rid of your last Club.

SHOWING A GREEN LIGHT

♠ 6 4 2
♡ 8 4 2
◇ A 9 8 5 2
♣ K Q

```
        N
   W         E
        S
```

♠ A 9 3
♡ A J 3
◇ Q J 10 3
♣ A J 5

You are South. The bidding:

North	East	South	West
No	No	1 ◇	1 ♡
3 ◇	No	3 N-T	All pass

West leads the ♡K, and East plays the Six.

WHAT DO YOU THINK OF YOUR SITUATION?

Your nine tricks are in sight—four Diamonds, three Clubs, and the Aces of the major suits. If West has the ◇K, all is well. But you ruefully reflect that you can't rely on that, and must try to find a line of play that allows for East getting the lead in Diamonds as well as for the likelihood that West bid on a five-card suit.

SO WHICH HEART DO YOU PLAY TO THE FIRST TRICK?

For a moment—but only for a moment—it may seem a good idea to duck and play the Three. But West, you realize, would fear a Bath Coup, and would almost certainly switch. You have little expectation that he would choose a minor suit, and Spades are every bit as dangerous to you as Hearts.

THEN DO YOU WIN WITH THE ACE?

That is just as bad; for if East gets the lead in Diamonds and has one Heart left to lead, West will reel off four Heart tricks.

SO WHAT DO YOU DO?

There is only one other card you can play—the Knave. And a very good card it is, too. For if you can't stand a Spade switch nor hope for a Club or a Diamond, the best thing to do is to encourage West to continue Hearts. And the drop of the Knave does just that. Not only does it banish his fear of a Bath Coup; it tells him that you now have only the bare Ace left, and that his partner still has two Hearts and so will have one to lead him after your Ace has been driven out. You, of course, know better. For if West had five Hearts, East started with only two; and if East turns out to have had three Hearts, then West had only four. So if he believes you and leads another Heart, your contract is safe. You win with the Ace, and take the Diamond finesse. If it fails, East cannot harm you, whether he has a Heart or not.

West quite probably will believe you, for from his point of view the fall of your Knave has every appearance of being an involuntary all-clear signal for his Hearts. And even if you hesitated, you haven't given the show away this time, since if you really had only the Ace-Knave, you might well ponder whether to take your Ace on the first or the second round.

HAND NO. 64
TROIKA

♠ J 5 4 3 2
♡ A J 5 2
◇ A K 9 3
♣ None

```
        N
    W       E
        S
```

♠ A Q 10 7
♡ Q 10 8 7
◇ J 5 4 2
♣ 5

You are South, and your contract is Six Spades. West leads the
♣K. A poor slam indeed. But don't waste mental energy on
accusing your partner or excusing yourself. It is not a hopeless
contract, though its chances of success amount to no more than
about 15 per cent. So you will need to be lucky and have all your
wits about you to take advantage of your luck. For one thing, the
patterns of your two hands—5-4-4-0 and 4-4-4-1—should warn
you to take every precaution you can against unbalanced
distributions of opponents' hands. You start on trumps, of course.

HOW DO YOU HANDLE THE SPADES?

You ruff the opening lead on the table and lead the ♠J. You have
to finesse, of course, and the lead of the Knave enables you to
pick up the missing trumps, even if East holds them all—
K-9-8-6.

Let us suppose East plays the Six and West the Eight. You
finesse again, East playing the Nine and West discarding a Club.
So now you are in the South hand with the ♠10. You draw the
last trump, East's King, with the Ace.

WHAT SUIT COMES NEXT AND WHY?

A careful inspection of the structure of your two side-suits tells you that you must tackle Hearts next. Good fortune has been with you so far; you have lost no trump trick. Much depends on how Hearts behave. If they are just as kind to you as Spades were, you have at your disposal a standard safety play in Diamonds to make sure of three tricks in that suit, which are all that you need; but if you lose a Heart, you will have to play for four tricks in Diamonds. So you must explore the Heart situation before starting on Diamonds.

WHICH HEART DO YOU LEAD?

The Ten. An honour must be led from the South hand, not a small card, so that you can pick up all West's Hearts if he should have four to the King-Nine; and you choose the Ten for psychological reasons. At this stage West cannot know what your distribution is: how many Diamonds you have and how many Diamond tricks you need. If he has several Hearts to the King, he may well argue that to cover your Ten would run the risk of dropping his partner's Queen and leaving the defence with no Heart trick at all. Therefore, if West does put his King on your Ten, you consider it quite likely that he is short-suited in Hearts —perhaps, even, the King is singleton. So if West covers and East follows suit when you win with the Ace, you cash the ♡J; and if the Ten is not covered and holds the trick, you follow up with the ♡Q. In those ways you give yourself the best chances of catching the ♡9.

We will assume that the ♡10 wins, but that West covers the ♡Q with the King, and when you put on dummy's Ace East fails to follow. You could go on to finesse against West's ♡9 and make four Heart tricks. But you don't.

WHY DON'T YOU?

Your slam is now a certainty, as you need lose only one Diamond with the safety-play of cashing the Ace and leading a small one to the Knave. But this means you must postpone finishing off the

♠ J 5 4 3 2
♡ A J 5 2
◇ A K 9 3
♣ None

♠ A Q 10 7
♡ Q 10 8 7
◇ J 5 4 2
♣ 5

Hearts. At the present moment you are on the table. If you returned to your own hand with a Spade to take the Heart finesse, you would have no trump left in either hand; and when the defence got the lead with the ◇Q, they could lead Clubs unhindered. So you tackle the Diamonds now and return to Hearts later to finesse for your four Heart tricks.

But suppose that you were not quite so lucky with the first two suits as you have been, and that you lost either a Spade or a Heart trick.

HOW DO YOU HANDLE THE DIAMONDS?

You now have to try to make four Diamonds. So you play the Ace. If the Queen should be dropped by East, you cross to the South hand with the Knave and, if necessary, finesse against the Ten. If the Queen does not drop to the Ace, you play the King, hoping to bring down the Queen on the second round. To handle Diamonds by leading the Knave on the first round and letting it run if West does not cover gives you a much poorer chance—mathematically not half as good—than cashing the Ace and King.

Playing this slam, with its three suits, was rather like driving over thin ice in a Russian sleigh drawn by three mettlesome horses abreast: you had to control each with dexterous technique —and the ice had to hold.

AN IMPOSSIBLE DISCARD

♠ A Q 10 4
♡ A K Q 6
◇ A K Q 5
♣ 3

```
        N
  W           E
        S
```

♠ K 9 5 2
♡ 7 5 4 2
◇ 7 6 4
♣ K 6

North-South vulnerable. You are South. The bidding:

North	East	South	West
2 ♣ (conventional)	5 ♣	Double	No
6 ♣	No	6 ♠	No
No	Double	All pass	

West leads the ♣8. East wins with the Ace and returns the ♣Q to your King, West following suit. Before you play from dummy you have quite a bit of thinking to do.

HOW MANY CERTAIN TRICKS HAVE YOU? AND WHAT DO YOU DEDUCE FROM THE BIDDING AND WEST'S OPENING LEAD?

Your certain tricks are four Spades, three Hearts, three Diamonds, and a Club—eleven in all. East's bidding showed a long Club suit, but he cannot have more than eight cards in it as West has played two Clubs. By leading a card of that suit West revealed that he did not regard the double as a Lightner lead-indicating

153

♠ A Q 10 4
♡ A K Q 6
◇ A K Q 5
♣ 3

♠ K 9 5 2
♡ 7 5 4 2
◇ 7 6 4
♣ K 6

double telling him not to lead his partner's suit. That decision of West's, you feel, most probably means that he has no more than one Spade, and that he therefore judged his partner's double to be based on a sure trump trick, especially as North's bidding had shown no length in any one suit. So West, you surmise, thought it best to try to give East a quick trick in Clubs—and succeeded. If the view you have taken is the right one, East has four Spades to the Knave.

WHERE, THEN, WILL YOU LOOK FOR YOUR TWELFTH TRICK?

Normally it could come from a 3–2 division of the outstanding Hearts, a 3–3 division of Diamonds, or from a ruff by the South hand. But if, as you so strongly suspect, there are four trumps in East's hand, the ruffing idea is out; and if West has only one Spade and two or three Clubs, then he has both red suits thoroughly stopped. To state your problem to yourself in that way is to suggest the solution. If West stops the two red suits, maybe he can be squeezed in them.

HOW AND WHEN COULD HE BE SQUEEZED?

At the sixth trick, after the two rounds of Clubs and three rounds of trumps, West's hand should consist of four Hearts to the Knave and four Diamonds to the Knave. A trump lead from the South hand will then squeeze him. If he discards a Heart, you make dummy's fourth Heart; if he discards a Diamond, you make dummy's fourth Diamond.

HOW DO YOU REACH THAT SQUEEZE POSITION?

There is only one way—by ruffing your ♣K in dummy at the second trick. If you were to discard a small card from either of dummy's red suits, you would be throwing away one of the menaces against West, and he could avoid being squeezed. Instead of discarding from dummy after West plays, as is the essence of your proposed squeeze, you would be discarding before him—several tricks before him, in fact. So as you clearly see that you cannot afford to part with either the ♡6 or the ◇5, you don't discard at all—you ruff; though actually you are, so to speak, 'discarding' a trump you don't need.

WHICH TRUMP DO YOU RUFF WITH?

The Ten, as it is obvious that to ruff with the Four would block the suit and allow East to get a ruff. Next, you cash the Ace and Queen of Spades, West failing on the second round, and lead the ♠4. This enables you to pick up East's trumps with the King-Nine in your own hand. At the sixth trick, you play the last Spade from your hand, drawing East's last trump and squeezing West in Hearts and Diamonds.

And so you make your slam—always provided, of course, that the hands you justifiably imagined for your opponents materialize in the play. You can't help it, for instance, if West is void of trumps and East has five. Now let us assume that you have guessed correctly the distribution of your opponents' hands.

CAN YOU MAKE THE SMALL SLAM IF YOU ARE IN NO-TRUMPS?

Quite impossible with any lead, provided West does not take the first round of Clubs, which, of course, he should not do, as he has no likely outside entry. For, as we have seen, it is only at the sixth trick, when he has nothing left but four Hearts or four Diamonds, that West can be squeezed by the lead of a winning Spade from the South hand. In short, there must be two rounds of Clubs to reach that position at the sixth trick, and here there has been only one round of Clubs and you dare not play another. Nor is there any other trick you can safely concede. So the count cannot be rectified, and West cannot be squeezed.

Curiously enough, if you are playing in Six Spades, it would be useless for East to duck the first Club. He would merely be giving you an over-trick, because you could ruff your losing Club with dummy's ♠10, and rectify the count that way.

HAND NO. 66
EXPLOITING THE UNKNOWN

♠ Q 10 7 3
♡ A K 6 4
◇ J 8 2
♣ A 4

```
        N
   W         E
        S
```

♠ A
♡ 9 8 7 5 2
◇ 7 4
♣ Q 8 6 3 2

Both vulnerable. You are South. The bidding:

East	South	West	North
1 N-T	No	No	Double
No	2 ♡	No	3 ♡
No	4 ♡	No	No
Double	All pass		

West leads the ♣10. Not a very attractive contract.

HOW DO YOU PLAY TO THE FIRST TRICK?

To judge from the lead and the bidding, the ♣K is with East; and it is obvious to you that you cannot afford to set up your ♣Q by playing low from dummy and letting East have the tricks He would, you fear, immediately switch to Diamonds; and thus having taken the first three tricks, would lean back complacently in his chair to wait for the setting trick in trumps to fall into his lap. So you decide to win the first trick with dummy's ♣A.

Agreed: but you are still left staring at your two losing Diamonds.

IS THERE ANY WAY OF RIDDING YOURSELF OF A LOSING DIAMOND?

The only possibility is to set up a master Spade in dummy, on which to throw a Diamond; and that must be done right away as you dare not part with the lead until it is done. The outstanding Spades are almost certainly divided 4–4, because with five or more West would have taken his partner's No-Trumps out into Two Spades, especially as he cannot have more than one Heart if East has the ♡Q guarded.

HOW, THEN, CAN YOU ESTABLISH A HIGH SPADE IN DUMMY?

There is no certain way, of course; all you can do is to try. There are two ways of making the attempt. Both are based on the likelihood of East having both the ♠K and the ♠J, on the hope that he doesn't hold the ♠9, and on the consideration that he cannot possibly be aware of the bareness of your ♠A. One way is to lead a small Spade from dummy. East, fearing that you have the Nine and intend to take the double finesse, may put in the Knave. If he does that, you return to the table with a Heart and lead the ♠Q. If East covers, you ruff, and dummy's ♠10 becomes the master Spade you want for a Diamond discard. If East does not cover, you discard a Diamond there and then. The second way is to lead dummy's ♠Q immediately—at the second trick. East covers, and your Ace wins. Dummy is entered with a Heart and a small Spade is led. There is a fair chance of East playing the Knave—for you to ruff.

WHICH OF THE TWO WAYS DO YOU PREFER?

There's very little in it, but the immediate lead of the Queen has the advantage of quite strongly suggesting that you have at least two Spades in your own hand. It is therefore perfectly logical for East to play the Knave on the second round rather than let you make your putative Nine, which, for all he can tell, may be the last Spade in your hand. The play of a small Spade from dummy has the psychological disadvantage of the natural tendency for second player to play low. This could result in East evading the trap almost automatically. On the whole, therefore, the immediate lead of the Queen is rather more likely to be successful.

HAND NO. 67
PHANTASM

♠ 10 9 3
♡ A J 4 2
♢ K Q
♣ A K 5 4

```
        N
  W          E
        S
```

♠ K 4
♡ K 10 9 7 5 3
♢ 8 7 3
♣ 10 2

Both vulnerable. You are South. The bidding:

West	North	East	South
1 ♠	Double	2 ♢	2 ♡
2 ♠	4 ♡	All pass	

West leads the ♢A and, when East plays the Four, switches to the ♣8, taken by the King on the table, East playing the Nine. You now draw trumps, of course.

WHICH OF DUMMY'S HEARTS DO YOU LEAD?

You are naturally going to win the first trick with either the Ace or the King. If both opponents follow, all is well. But if all three outstanding trumps should be in one hand, you have to guard against that hand being East's, since you cannot afford to let him get the lead and play a Spade through your King. If West should have all the trumps, that will not greatly matter; for you could strip Clubs and Diamonds from your two hands and then throw West in with his Queen of trumps when he must either play

Spades up to your King or give you a ruff-and-discard, It is therefore dummy's ♡A that you lead, so that if West fails to follow suit you will be able to pick up East's Queen.

But both follow all right, and the ♡Q drops from West.

IS THERE ANYTHING MORE TO BOTHER ABOUT?

At rubber bridge, as the contract has not been doubled or redoubled, you would now table your cards and claim your ten tricks—a Diamond and a Diamond ruff in dummy, two Clubs, and six trump tricks. But at duplicate, especially in a match-pointed pairs contest where it could gain you a top, it would be worth while having a shot for an over-trick.

WHERE COULD AN OVER-TRICK COME FROM?

If West has six Spades to the Ace-Queen-Knave—as he well may since he rebid the suit, though vulnerable, after the double and his partner's weak response and over your free bid of Hearts— there is a way in which you might succeed in persuading him to let you make your ♠K. Your line of reasoning is that West cannot know you have already fulfilled your contract, and therefore is probably still hoping to defeat you. But he does know that that can only happen if he manages to make three Spade tricks. So what you have to do is to make him think that you may have three Spades to lose.

HOW CAN YOU DO THAT?

By making a show of elimination play which you are careful, however, to stop just short of being complete. West's ♡Q dropped, you remember, to the third trick. At the fourth trick you draw East's last trump. You then cross to dummy with a Club and ruff a Club in your own hand. Returning to dummy with a Diamond, you ruff another Club. Eight tricks have now been played. Dummy's last five cards are his original three Spades and two trumps, while the South hand has its original King and Four of Spades, two trumps, and a Diamond. But you hope you have presented West with the illusion that your hand now consists of three Spades and two trumps. He won't place you with a Diamond, since you could have ruffed it in dummy. You now lead the ♠4, trusting that West is a good enough player to

♠ 10 9 3
♡ A J 4 2
◇ K Q
♣ A K 5 4

♠ K 4
♡ K 10 9 7 5 3
◇ 8 7 3
♣ 10 2

reason like this: 'South has three Spades, and if he is leading from the King, there's no defence that can defeat him. But if his three Spades are small ones, then, as I started with six, my partner must have the singleton King. If I play the ♠Q or ♠J, he will have to overtake in an eliminated situation and give the declarer a ruff-and-discard for his tenth trick. So I must go up with my Ace, crashing my partner's King. Then I hope to take two more Spade tricks with my Queen and Knave. The play cannot give the declarer his contract, for if his three Spades are headed by the King, he gets home anyway. It's the only chance of breaking him.' Do you remember that when you were defending in Hand No. 61, you rightly argued that way in a similar situation?

This and the previous hand are concerned with plays based on psychological factors. We have ended the book with them to emphasize how important psychology can be in the making and breaking of bridge contracts, though it figures so scantily in textbooks on card-play. The ability to exploit such plays stands high in the armoury of the successful bridge player. So our final word of advice is this slogan:

'Remember, nor does the enemy know everything!'